Bent Nails and Chipped Bricks

Rejected by Men, Selected by God

Bent Nails and Chipped Bricks

Rejected by Men, Selected by God

Jeffrey Reed

Treasure House

An Imprint of
Destiny Image‚ Publishers, Inc.
P.O. Box 310
Shippensburg, PA 17257-0310

"For where your treasure is
there will your heart be also." Matthew 6:21

ISBN 1-56043-265-9

For Worldwide Distribution
Printed in the U.S.A.

Treasure House books are available through these fine distributors outside the United States:

Christian Growth, Inc.
Jalan Kilang-Timor, Singapore 0315

Vine Christian Centre
Mid Glamorgan, Wales, United Kingdom

Rhema Ministries Trading
Randburg, South Africa

Omega Distributors
Ponsonby, Auckland, New Zealand

Salvation Book Centre
Petaling, Jaya, Malaysia

WA Buchanan Company
Geebung, Queensland, Australia

Successful Christian Living
Capetown, Rep. of South Africa

Word Alive
Niverville, Manitoba, Canada

Inside the U.S., call toll free to order:
1-800-722-6774
Or reach us on the Internet: **http://www.reapernet.com**

Contents

Chapter 1

David and the "Discarded Vessel"

avid faced one of the darkest moments of his life the day the Amalekites burned Ziklag, the place where David and his men had left their wives and children while they were away. Something happened in the traumatic hours of David's dark moment that is being resurrected and repeated by the Holy Ghost to bring deliverance to the Church in our day!

David's pain came from the past. The Amalekites were the very people that his pursuer, Saul, had been commanded by God to destroy years before. What the father wouldn't do, God raised up a son to do. After Saul failed to obey God, and then lied to Samuel about it, God commanded Samuel to anoint David the shepherd boy as king in Saul's place.

Now, after years of pursuit and life on the run, Saul's sin again caught up to David! This catastrophe not only threatened everything David loved and possessed, but also threatened to destroy the unity and love that bound his small army together—a relationship that had been won in the cave of Adullum through hardship and battle together!

And it came to pass, when David and his men were come to Ziklag on the third day, that the Amalekites had invaded the south, and Ziklag, and smitten Ziklag, and burned it with fire; and had taken the women captives, that were therein: they slew not any, either great or small, but carried them away, and went on their way. So David and his men came to the city, and, behold, it was burned with fire; and their wives, and their sons, and their daughters, were taken captives. Then David and the people that were with him lifted up their voice and wept, until they had no more power to weep. And David's two wives were taken captives, Ahinoam the Jezreelitess, and Abigail the wife of Nabal the Carmelite. And David was greatly distressed; for the people spake of stoning him, because the soul of all the people was grieved, every man for his sons and for his daughters: but David encouraged himself in the Lord his God (1 Samuel 30:1-6 KJV).

When David and his men found Ziklag destroyed by fire and their wives and sons and daughters taken captives, they "wept aloud until they had no strength left to weep" (1 Sam. 30:4). After David encouraged himself in the Lord, He sought counsel from the only trustworthy source in times of need.

And David said to Abiathar the priest, Ahimelech's son, I pray thee, bring me hither the ephod. And

Abiathar brought thither the ephod to David. And David inquired at the Lord, saying, Shall I pursue after this troop? shall I overtake them? And he answered him, Pursue: for thou shalt surely overtake them, and without fail recover all. So David went, he and the six hundred men that were with him, and came to the brook Besor, where those that were left behind stayed. But David pursued, he and four hundred men: for two hundred abode behind, which were so faint that they could not go over the brook Besor (1 Samuel 30:7-10 KJV).

Hidden in verse 11 is a powerful principle that will define the Lord's work in His Church well into the next century:

And they found an Egyptian in the field, and brought him to David, and gave him bread, and he did eat; and they made him drink water; and they gave him a piece of a cake of figs, and two clusters of raisins: and when he had eaten, his spirit came again to him: for he had eaten no bread, nor drunk any water, three days and three nights. And David said unto him, To whom belongest thou? and whence art thou? And he said, I am a young man of Egypt, servant to an Amalekite; and my master left me, because three days agone I fell sick (1 Samuel 30:11-13 KJV).

David and his band of angry rescuers were hot on the trail of a much larger group of armed kidnappers, but they really didn't know where they were going. When David's men found an abandoned, rejected slave who was nearly dead, David held up his 400-man raiding party to revive the man. For some reason, he saw value in this discarded slave, and after giving him food and drink, he personally invested time in him. In the end, David's investment in a rejected man became the key to total victory.

And David said to him, Canst thou bring me down to this company? And he said, Swear unto me by God, that thou wilt neither kill me, nor deliver me into the hands of my master, and I will bring thee down to this company. And when he had brought him down, behold, they were spread abroad upon all the earth, eating and drinking, and dancing, because of all the great spoil that they had taken out of the land of the Philistines, and out of the land of Judah. And David smote them from the twilight even unto the evening of the next day: and there escaped not a man of them, save four hundred young men, which rode upon camels, and fled. And David recovered all... (1 Samuel 30:15-18 KJV).*

The key to David's success in "recovering all" is found in the fact that he picked up an "abandoned vessel" who showed David where the Amalekites were feasting, dancing, and having a good time. The Lord told David to overtake the enemy, and He promised David he would "recover all" (1 Sam. 30:8). But the Lord didn't show David where to go right away. He was going to fulfill His promise through a broken and rejected vessel in need of rescue.

I want you to understand that as we close out this century and enter the twenty-first century, *God is on the search in the Church! He is looking for His vessels that have been abandoned and rejected. He is gathering to Himself the vessels that have been left behind, overlooked, and stepped on.* God has His search party looking for you! People like you are going to lead the Kingdom of God to victory in the years ahead! You and I have been picked up and restored by the Son of David! Our evil master had also rejected and discarded us in the wilderness of sin, but Jesus left the "ninety and nine" to find us, because He is out to recover all!

The Bible says David found this Egyptian man in the field where his master had abandoned him. Ironically, this abandoned and rejected vessel became the catalyst God used to boost His rejected leader to national prominence on one of Israel's darkest days! The very next chapter of First Samuel closes out the book with the sad story of Saul's death at the hands of the Philistines. The time had come for David to arise and assume the throne of Judah, and later, all of Israel. We have the task of glorifying our rejected King on His throne too!

I was constructing a home in the Mississippi area, and all of my workers had gone to lunch. I decided to stay at the site to do some things when I saw a gentleman approach me from out of nowhere, and he didn't look too well. Frankly, he didn't look like much. As a matter of fact, he looked like his elevator didn't reach the top floor. But he politely asked me, "Sir, do you have any cans on the back of your truck?" I told him,

"Well sir, I don't know. You can look back there and see." I watched him going through his motions, thinking that he wasn't someone you'd really pay any attention to normally. Most people would tend to look down their nose at him.

I watched him rummage through the bed of my truck and pick up a can that was crushed. It suddenly struck me that we go to a vending machine, put in two or three quarters, and press the button. Out comes the soda, and we drink the substance and throw the can away. We think we have drained all the value out of what we bought. The truth is that we fail to realize that there is more value in the can than there is in the substance! It took one whose "elevator doesn't reach the top floor" in the eyes of most people, to realize the obvious! We do the same thing with people in our society, and even in our churches! We evaluate and drain the "substance" out of them like soda cans, and once the thing we value is gone, we discard the rest. I watched the gentleman walk slowly down the road, stopping here and there to reach down into the ditch and to pick up discarded cans, or to pick up flattened cans that had been run over by cars.

A little later, another gentleman drove up to the job site and asked, "Pastor Reed, how do you like the columns on this house?" I hadn't paid any attention to the columns, so we began to look at them. The moment I realized that the columns in that house were made of aluminum, God began to give me a revelation! I began to realize that the entire house was supported and held

Chapter 2

Your Time Has Come!

This generation is facing a critical leadership deficit. The world system just can't produce the leaders we need for our day, and it is no accident. God ordained that *more than one deliverer* would come from Zion! The children of the Kingdom are destined to infiltrate every area of society in this hour. Redeemed sons and daughters of God are going to emerge as our mayors, presidents, senators, congressmen, and city council representatives. Like the first Cornerstone, these cornerstones of our society will be rejected stones who have been chosen by God and set in places of honor for such a time as this!

Our society is littered with alcoholics, drug dealers, substance abusers, misfits, juvenile delinquents, and social failures. You might not see much in them, but remember: God uses the scrap. He's looking through the graveyards of society to collect some of the sorriest samples of the living dead He can find. He has some glory He wants to drape around their decaying bodies.

He has some mercy and grace to apply to their broken lives. He's poking around in the desert among the abandoned rejects because He's planted deliverers among them! God is going to have the last say, the last laugh, and *all of the glory!*

Some time later, Jesus went up to Jerusalem for a feast of the Jews. Now there is in Jerusalem near the Sheep Gate a pool, which in Aramaic is called Bethesda and which is surrounded by five covered colonades. Here a great number of disabled people used to lie–the blind, the lame, the paralyzed. One who was there had been an invalid for thirty-eight years. When Jesus saw him lying there and learned that he had been in this condition for a long time, He asked him, "Do you want to get well?" "Sir," the invalid replied, "I have no one to help me into the pool when the water is stirred. While I am trying to get in, someone else goes down ahead of me." Then Jesus said to him, "Get up! Pick up your mat and walk." At once the man was cured; he picked up his mat and walked. The day on which it took place was a Sabbath, and so the Jews said to the man who had been healed, "It is the Sabbath; the law forbids you to carry your mat." He replied, "The man who made me well said to me, 'Pick up your mat and walk.' " So they asked him, "Who is this fellow who told you to pick it up and walk?" The man who was healed had no idea who it was, for Jesus had slipped away into the crowd that was there. Later Jesus found him at the temple and said to him, "See, you are well again. Stop sinning or something worse may happen to you." The man

Church! In one season you may be the discarded and empty can that needs to be "picked up and recovered." In the next season, He may send you as a column whose mission is to lift others up!

The important truth is that you can't get to the particular place of God's anointing unless someone else comes along and picks you up. *God knows how to pick you out of the "guttermost" and raise you to the uttermost!* God knows how you have been overlooked and passed over, but God simply says, "So? What does it matter? I've chosen him!" Other folks may not understand your worth and value, but you just look at them and say:

"So? I'm being transformed by the Master into a pillar of power! I might not be who or what you want me to be right now, but that doesn't matter! I might not be in the place you want me to be in right now, but that doesn't matter! I just need somebody to pick me up, somebody who supernaturally sees some worth in me. I know I'm on my way to someplace. My old master just left me abandoned in the field. He rejected me because in his eyes, all the 'good stuff' had been drained out of me. All the substance he thought was valuable had been spent, so he discarded the 'remains.' I wouldn't do what he wanted me to do. But I'm telling you—God is sending along a David in my life! He knows where I am, and He knows how to pick me up. I'm going to be just as faithful to my heavenly Master as I was to my previous master!"

together by the same material as the discarded cans my peculiar guest had collected earlier! Once we drained the "substance of value" from the cans, we threw them away. But another man saw the true value that remained in what we had discarded! Does this sound familiar? It should.

> *Jesus saith unto them, Did ye never read in the scriptures, The stone which the builders rejected, the same is become the head of the corner: this is the Lord's doing, and it is marvellous in our eyes?* (Matthew 21:42 KJV)

> *If so be ye have tasted that the Lord is gracious. To whom coming, as unto a living stone, disallowed indeed of men, but chosen of God, and precious, ye also, as lively stones, are built up a spiritual house, an holy priesthood, to offer up spiritual sacrifices, acceptable to God by Jesus Christ* (1 Peter 2:3-5 KJV).

You might feel like you've been in the ditches of life. Perhaps you feel rejected, dejected, overlooked, and abandoned. Listen: God will send you a man (if He hasn't already sent him to you). He will probably be someone who knows what it is like to be overlooked. God knows how to raise up folk that are voted the most unlikely to succeed in life. God knows how to put His hand on people that we look down our nose at. He loves to raise them up, so they can raise you up and pick you out of the field where folk have abandoned you! God may use you or me as a "soda can" one season, and in another He may install us as a pillar in His *went away and told the Jews that it was Jesus who had made him well* (John 5:1-15).

Last year, I had the privilege of taking my family to Disneyworld. The lines were unbelievable because we went during the peak season. It seemed like we had to wait forever to ride our favorite rides, but there is something unusual about those long waits. Even when we were still waiting some distance away in the back of the line, we could hear the screams and laughter of the people who were finally enjoying their turn. We stood in line for an hour or more for some of the rides, but once we reached the head of the line, we forgot about the long wait—it was *our turn*! There was nothing like it! Don't be shocked, but this is how it is in the Kingdom of God too.

You may feel like you've been "in the back of the spiritual line" for a lifetime! You can hear the shouts and sounds of joy of those who proceeded you. You're sure they are having a good time, and you don't really mind. You really want to rejoice with them, but you may be hurting so badly that you just want to ask, "God, when am I going to be blessed too? When are You going to lay Your hands on me? When are You going to touch me? Are You going to raise me up too?"

The Spirit of the Lord is declaring to you: "It is your turn to be blessed." It is no accident that you are reading these words right now. God establishes your steps if you delight in Him (see Ps. 37:23). This book is a written decree to those who are drawn by the Spirit to open its pages: *This is your year of jubilee!* You may have been down and out, but God has just walked onto the scene with His hand extended to you! This is a holy season of restoration for your life!

> *And ye shall hallow the fiftieth year, and proclaim liberty throughout all the land unto all the inhabitants thereof: it shall be a jubile unto you; and ye shall return every man unto his possession, and ye shall return every man unto his family. A jubile shall that fiftieth year be unto you: ye shall not sow, neither reap that which groweth of itself in it, nor gather the grapes in it of thy vine undressed* (Leviticus 25:10-11 KJV).

Jesus had come to Jerusalem to observe a Jewish feast the day He walked near the Sheep Gate and saw the paralyzed man at the pool of Bethesda. This picture of Jesus coming to Jerusalem is a type and shadow of Jesus coming to the Church. The pool near the Sheep Gate was called *Bethesda* in Aramaic, and it means "mercy." It was surrounded by five covered columns or porches (the number five is often symbolic of grace or favor in the Bible). When Jesus the Good Shepherd walked past the Sheep Gate and entered the pool of mercy, it was as if God had come into His Church. He fills it with mercy and surrounds it with grace. This is described in the Book of Lamentations:

> *Because of the Lord's great love* [mercies—KJV] *we are not consumed, for His compassions never fail. They are new every morning; great is Your faithfulness* (Lamentations 3:22-23).

The Psalmist tells us, "Love and faithfulness meet together; righteousness and peace kiss each other" (Ps. 85:10). It is because of God's mercy that you are reading these words, and it is because of His mercy that you and I are where we are right now! God has allowed us to hang around here for the last part of the twentieth century so we could hear His proclamation to the Church: "It is your time to be blessed." We also need to understand that the only reason it is "our time to be blessed" is because we are surrounded with the mercies of God.

Now there is in Jerusalem near the Sheep Gate a pool, which in Aramaic is called Bethesda and which is surrounded by five covered colonades. Here a great number of disabled people used to lie–the blind, the lame, the paralyzed (John 5:2-4).

This pool was perhaps the only place where people could witness a miracle in those days. Until John the Baptist arrived, Israel hadn't heard the voice of a prophet or witnessed a miracle for hundreds of years—except for the occasional miracle of healing at the pool of mercy near the Sheep Gate. An angel would stir the waters in the pool, and whoever entered the waters first would be healed of his infirmity.

We have a lot of mercy and grace in the Church, but have you noticed that we still have a lot of spiritually disabled people too? Too many of us have been focusing our attention and faith on the occasional stirring of the water. God is getting ready to turn our gaze directly to Him because He wants to raise us up!

The Bible lists three categories of people among the great number of disabled people who used to wait for the waters to be stirred: the blind, the halt or the lame, and the paralyzed. When the Scriptures talk about the blind, it may refer to individuals who can't see, or it may refer to individuals who can't *perceive what God is saying to them* for one reason or another.

Have you ever been so "down" that you didn't want to hear what God was saying? Knowing how He often speaks through people who love you, you held on to your pain and refused to listen to what your husband or wife said. You also ignored what your best friend said because you were in a "down time." God says people in this state are "blind." Even though we are sometimes blind to the truth because of our pain or stubbornness, we still tend to stay around the "pool" (the Church). Your pastor preached twice every Sunday, trying to stir the waters for you. You went to every Bible study you could, but you weren't getting anything out of it. At least you were *waiting* for God by the pool.

> *...those who hope in* [wait upon—KJV] *the Lord will renew their strength. They will soar on wings like eagles; they will run and not grow weary, they will walk and not be faint* (Isaiah 40:31).

As long as you remain in His house, and stay in the presence of God, *your turn will come* after a while. The Bible says that not only were the blind there, but the lame were gathered at the pool of mercy. The lame may either be the physically handicapped who are unable to walk, or those who are unable to "walk out" the commandments of God. Have you ever made up your mind "to do right"? You made a vow to yourself and walked out the door and promptly fell. After you picked up yourself and your broken vow, you told yourself, "Tomorrow I'm going to do better." It seemed like the next day you fell even harder. The process seems to be eternal, and life like an unending series of stumbles and falls, ups and downs, ins and outs. Listen my friend, it is your turn to be blessed!

You may be ready to give up and throw in the towel, but God is coming to rescue you. You don't have to quit—just hold on and look up! Your self-esteem may be at an all-time low, but God is going to build it up on a more sure foundation. You may feel down and out, like you are doomed to be a lifetime loser and outcast, but God has come to lift you up. Your chips may be down, but God is going to pick you up. You feel so low that your life is in the gutter right now. Take heart. God is going to get you out of that gutter right now!

That paralyzed man didn't have a lot going for him, but he did one thing right! He made sure he was planted next to the only source of miracles he could find! Maybe he had failed to be the first incurable case into the pool of mercy for 35 years, but at least his faith was strong enough to keep him in the house of miracles. I'm telling you—no matter how low or hopeless your situation may be as you read these words—at least you are in the Church. I don't care how disabled you are. You've hung around here long enough for your turn to come around! God says it is your turn to be blessed. He knows your pain and your infirmity, but He has something to say about you: "Those that be planted in the house of the Lord shall flourish in the courts of our God" (Ps. 92:13 KJV). This is the promise of the Church. It may look like you won't blossom for a long time, but you just tell yourself: "It's my time now!"

> *The Spirit of the Lord God is upon me; because the Lord hath anointed me to preach good tidings unto the meek...to appoint unto them that mourn in Zion, to give unto them beauty for ashes, the oil of joy for mourning, the garment of praise for the spirit of heaviness; **that they might be called trees of righteousness,** the planting of the Lord, that He might be glorified* (Isaiah 61:1a,3 KJV).

You are a tree of righteousness (not your righteousness—*His* righteousness). You thought your success or failure was up to you, but God Himself has dug around your roots and fertilized the soil. The divine husbandman is removing the weeds around you that seem to be choking out your life and fruitfulness. In your eyes, nothing good was being produced in your life, and you got down on your blessings. Don't be deceived: God didn't forget about you. He didn't overlook you. God is saying it is your turn now!

In days gone by, you might have been up and down, and in and out. Now God has turned your season around because you kept trying. It is your turn now to be blessed. The Bible also says that there were paralyzed people waiting around the pool of mercy. Another term, "withered," refers to those whose hands were paralyzed or handicapped. They could not work with God. Shepherds quickly learn to recognize these conditions among the people in the house of God. We see the blind sheep hurting in the pews while the Word flows past unseeing eyes and deaf ears, yet we hope and pray that somehow they will receive and be healed. We preach to people who are up and down, who stumble numbly through life, and we want to give them a support or a crutch to help them further down the road. We see people who clearly have great potential, but their hands and hearts are withered.

It may be difficult for you to understand what a shepherd feels when he or she sees you in these conditions, but God is telling us to put our backs to the plow and preach and minister even harder! We have a holy commission to declare the truth: Deliverance has come to Zion! Your Great Shepherd is walking through the sheep gate right now! He has stirred this preacher from Mississippi to tell you in black and white: *It is your turn to be blessed!*

The handicapped people who were sprawled helplessly around the pool of mercy in the Book of John are a picture of people in the Church. They had circled the pool of mercy, and they were surrounded by grace, but they still had a crippling condition! They were paralyzed, lame, and hopelessly blind. The only thing they had going for them was that they were waiting for a miracle of mercy. I like people like that. You might be blind, but you are still waiting. You might be paralyzed and hurting, but you are still waiting. You might be withered, but you are still waiting.

Listen, if you have the courage to wait upon the Lord, then you will activate God's Word. He has declared the outcome in advance! You don't have to have a degree in biblical Hebrew and Greek to understand God's promise: "Wait for the Lord; be strong and take heart and wait for the Lord" (Ps. 27:14). Isaiah the prophet declared, "...those who hope in [wait upon—KJV] the Lord will renew their strength. They will soar on wings like eagles; they will run and not grow weary, they will walk and not be faint" (Is. 40:31).

People may have overlooked us because we have been down, but just *wait*. People have stepped on us and abused us, but just *wait*. Don't let anybody entice you or drive you away from the pool! Don't let anybody or any situation pull you away from the house of mercy! You and I have to stay planted right there in Zion. We have to think of ourselves as trees planted by the rivers of water. Most of us act like we're potted plants. If things are not going too well over here, we'll move over there. If things are not going well over there, we will move even further over there. Your time is about to come up. God is getting ready to bless you. The oil has been poured on the head of the High Priest of our souls, but you have to stay in line and remain in the place He has planted you until the oil comes to you.

What Happens When Mercy Walks In?

The Gospel of John tells us that the people gathered around the pool of Bethesda had placed their hope in the pool. They were looking to the pool of mercy for their miracle, and they had no idea that something better was about to enter the place. The pool of Bethesda represented mercy. The few chance encounters with God that happened there each year were just temporary and limited glimpses of the glory that was destined to come to all.

Something better was about to come along, and this greater miracle is what the Book of Hebrews is all about. Until the day Jesus walked in, the pool of mercy was the point of contact where only one particular individual at one particular time would contact the miraculous when an angel of God would trouble the water. The first one to step into the water was healed, while the others who were left behind watched in even greater pain as he shouted and thanked God for his healing. When something better comes on the scene, it is time to take your hope away from the pool and look at Mercy Himself!

That day when Jesus entered the area of the pool of Bethesda, mercy left the pool and began to walk bodily before the hurting. As always, Jesus came to take their attention off of the pool and show them that mercy is no longer in the pool; Mercy Himself was *standing in their midst*! His reception was predictable. The Bible says, "He came unto His own, and His own received

Him not" (Jn. 1:11 KJV). Even today, most people don't realize or accept the fact that Mercy has left the pool and He is walking right in the middle of His Church. Most of us act like God only has a few privileged favorites who get their prayers answered and who are worthy to be used in His Kingdom.

It is one thing to go to a miraculous pool to get healed, but the truth is that the Miracle-worker of the pool has *come to you*! You've been down so long that you think you need to "go somewhere" and "find somebody else" with a touch of the anointing to find deliverance. I'm telling you by the Holy Ghost: you are reliving the miracle of the pool of Bethesda right now, right where you are! God is saying this is your year of jubilee! The debts and misfortunes of years gone by have been washed away by the blood of the Sacrificed Lamb. You know how hard it seemed when you prayed and prayed and kept on knocking, but nothing seemed to open up. Well, God has brought the Source of healing water to you!

Mercy is walking past the "sheep gate" where you live; He is searching for you among the hopeful and hopeless. Mercy and truth have kissed each other, and truth has sprung up out of the earth. The curtain of separation has been torn; the veil that barred the crippled and the infirm from God's presence has been rent. Mercy has walked out of the Holy of Holies along the same path that Truth walked before the veil of separation was torn. Mercy descended to the tomb where Truth was buried and sat down. Three days later, Truth sprang up from the earth and joined His arms with Mercy. Thus our mercy and truth met together in Christ Jesus. Now, God says it is your turn to be blessed!

Why is God declaring that He is getting ready to bless you? Mercy and truth have met together! Righteousness and peace have kissed each other! What used to be against you—the very blemish that banned you from serving Him—has now become the reason He is searching for you! It is time to move. You need to get ready to pick up and carry away the very thing that has held you down so long! *The symbol of your captivity and handicap is destined to become a badge of deliverance under your arm!*

Do you know what I'm doing here? I'm not trying to get you happy, I'm trying to get you healed! I'm trying to get you to be a holistic individual. Sometimes the saints of God stagger through life because they are out of balance. It seems if we are anointed to minister to others, we're broke. If we are halfway prosperous, we're also carnal or physically sick ourselves! God wants you to be holistic. Jesus put it this way: "The thief comes only to steal and kill and destroy; I have come that they [the sheep] may have life, and have it *to the full*" (Jn. 10:10). When Jesus said "life to the full," He was saying He wants you to be healthy, wealthy, and anointed.

The devil has tried to hold us down like the man at the pool of mercy who had been an invalid for 38 years (see Jn. 5:5). I don't know how long you've been in your condition, but many times these conditions have time periods attached to them. Lazarus was in the grave for four days before the word of the Lord came to him and raised him up (see Jn. 11:39-44). The woman with the issue of blood suffered for 12 years, but her day of deliverance came when the word of the Lord dried up her condition and renewed her life (see Lk. 8:43). Another woman was "bent over" for 18 long years, but the day came when the word of the Lord straightened her back and restored her God-given dignity (see Lk. 13:11-13).

Everyone who knew Lazarus had already disposed of his remains. They had put him out of sight and buried him. His closest friends and family loved him, but they had already thrown dirt on him. You may be in the same condition: maybe even the people who love you the most just don't see any usefulness left in you; they can't visualize any good in you. Maybe there is nothing about you that others value or desire. Have others thrown dirt over your fallen body and forgotten you?

Jesus hasn't forgotten about you. He is standing at your grave right now. If you listen, you will hear Him speak the word over your life and call your name out loud! There is a time period attached to your situation. You know you are not where you were destined to be. You know you don't have what you really desire. All of your God-given dreams have not yet been fulfilled, your heavenly vision hasn't come to pass yet!

God is declaring it is your turn now to be blessed. Your dream is going to come to pass. Your heavenly vision is about to kiss the earth and be revealed in your year of jubilee! When you can see yourself through the eyes of God, then you will rise up and do something. Jesus knew that the man at the pool had been there for a long time. Knowledge like this can dampen human faith and halt the miraculous, but Jesus was unmoved by time. It doesn't matter how long you've been on the bottom, when Jesus calls you forth, you are destined to rise again!

How many times do you think people accidentally stepped on that paralyzed and helpless man? How many times was he run over in the rush for a miracle in the pool of mercy? How many times did somebody drop him while trying to get him into the pool? By the time Jesus walked onto the scene, the man had no one left to help him. Perhaps his parents were dead, and his brothers and sisters had forgotten him as a hopeless case. Whatever happened in the past was forgotten the moment Jesus asked the man the most important question of his life: "Do you want to get well?" (Jn. 5:6b)

I'm asking you the same question right now! It may be the most important question in your life too. Answer from the heart, not your head: Do you want to get well? Do you want to be whole and free?

You may have been stuck in your hopeless condition for a long time, but God is raising you up. He is setting you in place because it is your time, child of God. God is come, and Mercy Himself has stepped out beside the pool of the Church. He declares today that it is your turn to be blessed! Jesus told the paralytic man, "Pick up your mat and walk" (Jn. 5:8b). God wants you to pick up every badge or outer symbol of your bondage and pain, and openly carry it out of the house of grace and mercy! Once He has cured you, He wants you to carry your deliverance in plain sight for all to see—no matter how it is received and perceived.

Chapter 3

Bent Nails and the King's Table

We serve an awesome God who foresees all things. God sees something when man sees nothing. When Samuel the prophet and the family of Jesse only saw a lowly shepherd boy, God saw a king (see 1 Sam. 16:1-13). The trick is coming to the place where we can see ourselves through the eyes of God.

Would you say the man who was attacked by thieves and rescued by the "Good Samaritan" was "half dead" or "half alive" when he was found? God didn't see him as "half dead." He was a man who was "half alive" and in need of a miracle. If you think you are "half dead," then you have to admit that you're still half alive and in need of a miracle too! No matter what the world has called you, God sees another side to you.

The sins of Saul brought about his own sudden destruction, along with the deaths of his sons. It also left his innocent grandson alone and crippled in a hostile world. Mephibosheth was well acquainted with lost potential and the sorrow of a future lost:

> *And Jonathan, Saul's son, had a son that was lame of his feet. He was five years old when the tidings came of Saul and Jonathan out of Jezreel, and his nurse took him up, and fled: and it came to pass, as she made haste to flee, that he fell, and became lame. And his name was Mephibosheth* (2 Samuel 4:4 KJV).

The long-forgotten son of Jonathan is reintroduced to David after Saul's death. Mephibosheth was a royal prince and the grandson of the king. He was the son of Jonathan, the deceased heir apparent to the throne of Israel, yet he now lived in the household of another:

> *And the king said, Is there not yet any of the house of Saul, that I may shew the kindness of God unto him? And Ziba said unto the king, Jonathan hath yet a son, which is lame on his feet. And the king said unto him, Where is he? And Ziba said unto the king, Behold, he is in the house of Machir, the son of Ammiel, in Lodebar. Then king David sent, and fetched him out of the house of Machir, the son of Ammiel, from Lodebar. Now when Mephibosheth, the son of Jonathan, the son of Saul, was come unto David, he fell on his face, and did reverence. And David said, Mephibosheth. And he answered, Behold thy servant! And David said unto him, Fear not: for I will surely shew thee kindness for Jonathan thy father's sake, and will restore thee all the land of Saul thy father; and thou shalt eat bread at my table continually. And he bowed himself, and said,*

What is thy servant, that thou shouldest look upon such a dead dog as I am? (2 Samuel 9:3-8 KJV)

The Bible makes it clear that Mephibosheth was dropped due to no fault of his own. He was removed from his inheritance because his grandfather sinned before God. He was dropped and permanently crippled because somebody else made a mistake and moved too fast at the wrong time, leaving Mephibosheth to pay for her mistake the rest of his life! He was to discover that God had already provided for him through a covenant that may have been made before Mephibosheth was even born!

When David received the crown of Judah at Hebron, God reminded him of the covenant he had made with Jonathan years before. Mephibosheth was Jonathan's only living descendent, and the sole direct heir of the covenant. When you enter into a covenant, you never do it just for yourself. You establish a covenant for your children and your children's children. The only way David could honor Jonathan's memory and fully observe the covenant was to find Jonathan's heir. That is why he asked his aides if there were any survivors of the house of Saul that he could show kindness to *for Jonathan's sake.*

Do you feel handicapped by circumstances over which you have no control? Do you look back to the past and ask, "How in the world did I allow myself to get in that condition?" God knows how long you have been in your condition. He also knows that nobody on earth but you really understands how that condition is working on you. Did you know that Jesus "took the drop" for you? He took your place when sin wanted to destroy your destiny. God knew you were going to be in your condition because He is a God of foreknowledge, who knows the end from the beginning (see Is. 46:10).

God is searching throughout His Church for somebody to whom He can show His kindness! He is out to honor His covenant with His Son, and with those who dare to dwell under the New Covenant established through the blood of the Lamb. He is looking for an heir through Christ who needs some mercy. He is freely bestowing His grace on the children of His covenant wherever He finds them. He is looking for someone who longs for His favor and divine touch.

Mephibosheth became lame in both of his feet when his nurse dropped him in his early years. Evidently his handicap was so severe that he couldn't walk at all (see 2 Sam. 19:26). The accident left him totally dependent on others for the rest of his life. His feet were turned in, crooked, and paralyzed. When King David called for him, Mephibosheth was living in a place called *Lodebar*, which means "no pasture." The area around Lodebar must have been incapable of supporting livestock or growing crops. Mephibosheth had somehow ended up in the home of a man named *Machir*, which means "salesman." Machir may have been using the prince's name to enhance his sales business in that barren area. Has the devil made a profit on your life? Has your life been used to benefit the selfish desires of others? You are the son of the King, yet you are lame in your feet, and it isn't your fault!

The devil has been making merchandise out of the King's sons, but now there is a King who is calling you to His table! I know you have been in Lodebar a long time. You haven't seen a rich pasture in a long time, but never forget that the Lord is your Shepherd! Even King David had to remind himself at times. The Almighty God is calling you to His table:

The Lord is my shepherd; I shall not want. He maketh me to lie down in green pastures: He leadeth me beside the still waters. He restoreth my soul: He leadeth me in the paths of righteousness for His name's sake. Yea, though I walk through the valley of the shadow of death, I will fear no evil: for Thou art with me; Thy rod and Thy staff they comfort me. Thou preparest a table before me in the presence of mine enemies: Thou anointest my head with oil; my cup runneth over. Surely goodness and mercy shall follow me all the days of my life: and I will dwell in the house of the Lord for ever (Psalm 23 KJV).

You have been dropped and then abandoned in Lodebar, but God is calling you out of your barren wilderness. You have been abused by the enemy, but God is calling you out of there. You have been mistaken for a homeless beggar without an inheritance, and you have been overlooked by those who manipulated you, but God is calling you out! You have been picked on and ridiculed by young and old, but God is calling you out of there. You have been rolled over and stepped on by careless and uncaring feet, but God is calling you out. You have been kicked around like a homeless son, and dropped in haste, but God is calling you out of there.

"Come here, Mephibosheth." Do you want to know what Mephibosheth thought of himself after all those years of abuse? Look at the words that spilled out of his heart when he bowed down on the floor before King David: "What is your servant, that you should notice a dead dog like me?" (2 Sam. 9:8b) This is one of the lowest terms a Jewish man could use for himself, especially since anything dead is considered ceremonially unclean and unworthy before God. Dead things were dragged away from the living and buried, and anyone who had touched something that was dead was required to stay separate from the community until he was ceremonially clean.

I like what David did. When Mephibosheth came into his presence David said, "Mephibosheth!" (see 2 Sam. 9:6). How many people have tried to separate you from your real name by calling you evil names that framed their low opinion of your worth or their jealousy toward you? Mephibosheth was forced out of the king's palace and into a huckster's household in a dry and lifeless place. He must have heard countless insults designed to put down his royal heritage and aggravate the pain of his handicap and disinheritance as the son of a dead prince from a displaced royal household.

Can you imagine how refreshing it was for Mephibosheth to hear the king speak his name with honor, affection, and respect after decades of abuse? The Son of David knows your name, too. He always calls you by your real name, the name tied to your true destiny. He knows your name means something, and He knows your name is precious. You may have been called ugly, fat, skinny, short, or tall; you may have been called a lot of evil things that were meant to pull you away from the destiny and honor ordained for your true name. Take heart. Just as David said, "Mephibosheth!" God is also calling you by your real name.

David said, "Mephibosheth!" "Your servant," he replied. "Don't be afraid," David said to him, "for I will surely show you kindness for the sake of your father Jonathan. I will restore to you all the land that belonged to your grandfather Saul, and you will always eat at my table." Mephibosheth bowed down and said, "What is your servant, that you should notice a dead dog like me?" Then the king summoned Ziba, Saul's servant, and said to him, "I have given your master's grandson everything that belonged to Saul and his family. You and your sons and your servants are to farm the land for him and bring in the crops, so that your master's grandson may be provided for. And Mephibosheth, grandson of your master, will always eat at my table"... (2 Samuel 9:6b-10).

This is your year of jubilee! The same God who called Samuel, Moses, Saul, and the 12 apostles of the Lamb by name, is now calling out *your name!* Mephibosheth was probably afraid that his grandfather's old enemy was looking for revenge, but the king's words immediately reassured him: "Don't be afraid...for I will surely show you kindness for the sake of your father Jonathan. I will restore to you..." (2 Sam. 9:7). He was telling Mephibosheth, "Your father and I *made a covenant* years ago. You weren't even born yet, but you were in the loins of your father." This meant that under the laws and customs of the Middle East, Mephibosheth, the handicapped and abandoned son of a deceased man, had the legal right to say, "Because you made a covenant with Daddy, King David, then you made a covenant with me too! I was in his loins and the blood of my father flows through my veins. What is mine is yours, and what is yours is mine!"

Middle Eastern covenants are *blood covenants.* The life is in the blood, and the family line is in the blood. Even the earthly heritage of Jesus Christ was carefully traced through the bloodline of his parents to conform to ancient prophecy. When Abraham met Melchizedek, the priest of the Most High and the king of Salem (peace), he paid tithes to him (see Gen. 14:18-20). The Book of Hebrews declares that Levi was in his loins! When Abraham stretched out his hands, then in the eyes of God, Levi in the loins of Abraham stretched out his hands and paid tithes also (see Heb. 7:9)! This is why the Melchizedek priesthood is greater than the Aaronic priesthood.

According to the writer of the Book of Hebrews, even the Aaronic priesthood (resident in the loins of

Abraham) bowed down to the priesthood of Melchizedek and paid tithes to him. That is why the Bible says the priesthood of Jesus didn't come through the order of the Aaronic priesthood; it is rooted in the order of the Melchizedek which is a priesthood forever and ever (see Heb. 7:11-28).

David made a promise to Mephibosheth. He was saying, "Listen, Mephibosheth. I know you're used to living in Lodebar, but I want you to eat with my sons and family at the king's table *continually*" (that means "around the clock, never-ending, never ceasing"). Unfortunately, Mephibosheth still had a problem with his legs. He was still lame. But let me point out something to you: What do you think Mephibosheth looked like when he put those two lame legs under the king's table and sat there eating like a child of the king? For one thing, nobody could tell he was lame! His handicap was covered by the king's provision! The second thing is even more important: Mephibosheth was sitting in a place of honor along with all of David's young princes. The forgotten prince was once again restored to royal honor as a royal prince of a royal household!

The same thing is happening to you and me and to millions of other believers in Zion right now! Our broken feet of human failure, the source of our rejection, have been placed under the King's table where they are covered *continually* by the King's provision. When I look at you as you dine among the princes of God, I can't know what you've been through. I can't see that personal side of you, and I can't blame you for your failures and sin. You are sitting at the king's table, and your brokenness has been forever covered by His table of provision!

I'm telling you that this is your time to be blessed. God is raising you up and setting you in a place of royal honor. It's your time as a child of God. God is come, and Mercy has stepped down by the pool and stepped into the Church! He is saying to you, "It is your turn to be blessed."

One time, I went to meet a building inspector at a work site where my construction company was working on a house in Mississippi. He told me, "Jeff, everything is looking fine. You have built everything to code. But I would like you to put some more hurricane straps on it."

Hurricane straps bind a house to its foundation when strong winds blow through during the hurricane season in coastal Mississippi. Houses aren't designed and built for sunny weather; they are designed to withstand the pressures and stress of stormy weather. Hurricane straps are metal bands that literally go over the top of a house and attach to anchor bolts in the foundation.

My problem was that the sheetrock couldn't go up on the interior walls until these hurricane straps were all in place. That meant I had to do the job myself since I'd sent all of my workers to lunch for the inspection. My second problem was that I needed some nails to put on those hurricane straps, and I didn't have any. I could have easily gone to the store and bought some new nails, but as I walked through the house, I noticed there were nails all over the floor.

I thought, "Why should I go to the store and buy new nails when there are old nails all over the floor!" When I bent down to pick up these nails, I realized that a lot of them were bent. My carpenters must have thrown them away because they didn't want to take the time to straighten them out and use them in the wall. I had already made up my mind not to get new nails, and besides, the old nails were made of the same material as the new nails. All they needed was somebody who would take the time to pick them up and straighten them out.

As I gathered up the bent nails in that place, I suddenly realized that God knows how to send people along to pick us up and straighten us out too. God wants some "hurricane straps" in His House too, and He doesn't want to use new nails either. For some unknown reason, God likes to use the "used stuff" that has been dropped, stepped on, discarded, and kicked around. He is perfectly willing to patiently sift through the dirt and debris to find people that men have overlooked, passed over, and looked down on, because He loves to exalt the humble and confound the wise.

When I began to pick up those nails, I discovered that some straight nails were mixed in the dirt with the bent nails. There are a lot of good people in the Church and in the world who were just dropped into some bad situations. I also noticed that a large number of nails were hidden even deeper under the layers of dust and grime. Fortunately, God knows how to reach out in time to raise us up—no matter how difficult it is, how deep we're buried, or how crooked we've become.

The hammer of the Word of God can straighten out any nail! You are made of the same material as "new nails" right out of the box, and God is saying, "I want to use you in my wall." Your hour has come. I don't know what you've been through already, and I don't know what you're going to go through, but I do know that God is out to pick you up and straighten you out for His glory!

It is at this awkward point that many people will fail to understand your predicament. You are between "here" and "there." People don't like change. Once they are accustomed to calling you a bent nail, and once they have seen you in the dirt, they expect you to stay there. If you move, you upset the order of things. God is out to upset the order of everything because He has a Kingdom to build. When people are upset at seeing you sitting with the King's sons, tell them, "So? Talk to God about it." When people look down their nose at you because you still have some dust and a crooked stretch in your appearance, just tell them, "So? I'm in the Master Builder's hands. He's straightening me out with the hammer of His Word. Haven't you heard? I'm going to be part of the wall of His House!"

It is impossible for most people to understand that you are a "soda can" on your way to becoming a pillar in the House of God. They will be uncomfortable with the news, because in their minds, once all of the "substance" was taken from you, you should have been perfectly content to be discarded for something or someone new. Fortunately, God's thoughts are higher than those of men. When other people want to rehearse all your downfalls and shortcomings, you should say, "So? Have you heard what God says about me?"

As I began to attach those vital hurricane straps to the wall of that house with those recovered and straightened nails, I could almost hear each nail say, "Thank you. The carpenters passed over me, the bricklayers walked by me, the owners kicked me around, and the plumbers didn't recognize my worth, but you picked me up. Thank you. The cement finishers abused me, and the carpenters discarded me as useless, but I'm glad you recognized my worth. Thank you!"

God sees something in you that nobody else can see. He saw something in you that made it worth His time to straighten you out for His holy service. He knew you would make it because He saw something on the inside of you that would fulfill His plans one day! His wall can't really be finished until you are in the wall. You were holding up the building program. God is really telling you that the Church cannot be completely finished until you are picked up and straightened out! Praise God He is into recycling!

When God walks in the Church, He sees a lot of bent nails. Sometimes the devil is telling Him to throw them away because they're not good for anything anymore. He says, "Look at them! They are all paralyzed, withered, and blind!" God just tells him, "I don't throw away scraps." God reaches down where you are and picks you up. Then He uses the hammer of His Word to straighten you out and put you in the wall of life. I can almost hear Him say, "Son, those nails were walked on all right, but they had a turn coming. They were dropped, but they had a turn coming. They were abused and kicked around, but they had a turn coming." If you haven't received the word of the Lord for your situation yet, let me share with you again: "This is your year of jubilee. God is going to release you and set you on high because He sees something in you that He can use. It is your turn to be blessed."

God doesn't throw away scraps. Every time He multiplied bread to feed the thousands who followed Him, He always had the nerve to say, "Gather up the fragments." Although other people think you are a worthless fragment that should be discarded, God has the nerve to say, "Gather him up. Gather her up. Gather up *all* of the fragments." You might be a "leftover," but you are going to be used by God.

The Lord is scouring the deserts of the wilderness and the dusty floors of His Church for the "last" remnant of the rejected. The One who declared that, "the last shall be first, and the first shall be last" (see Lk. 13:30), knows you have been down. He can see the condition of your broken heart and shattered life, but it doesn't matter to Him. The table is prepared, and His house is waiting for you to take your place of destiny. Life is about to change because the Master is bending down to pick you up!

Chapter 4

Rejected by Man but Selected by God

istorians and biblical scholars say Jesus never traveled more than 150 miles from His home, yet He somehow duplicated Himself in 12 disciples and reached the entire world! David did the same thing on a smaller scale hundreds of years before that. Somehow we need to recapture and restore the secret of leadership that Jesus used to set the world on fire in only three years of ministry. We need to rediscover the principles that catapulted David the shepherd from a cave hideout to the throne of Israel!

> *David left Gath and escaped to the cave of Adullam. When his brothers and his father's household* [family] *heard about it, they went down to him there. All those who were in distress or in debt or discontented gathered around him, and he became their leader. About four hundred men were with him* (1 Samuel 22:1-2).

David somehow transformed those 400 rejects who joined him in the cave of Adullam. He did something to change the men society had labeled as "losers" into winners. They came to him distressed, discontented, and in debt; but somehow David put himself into them, and together they conquered nations, destroyed giants, overcame kingdoms, and eventually conquered most of the known world! By the time David's son, Solomon, came to the throne, the Bible says Solomon had "rest from all his enemies" (1 Chron. 22:9). This gave Solomon the freedom and resources to build God a house. It almost seems like David had a divine copy machine that let him produce duplicates of himself. This is the pattern of God.

God loves to duplicate Himself in His creation, and especially in the human race. Duplication is the miracle of the cave of Adullam that transformed beaten, hopeless men into fearless warriors and enabled them to capture kingdoms. Jesus told His disciples, "What I tell you in the dark, speak in the daylight; what is whispered in your ear, proclaim from the roofs" (Mt. 10:27). Paul echoed Jesus when he told his disciple, Timothy, "And the things you have heard me say in the presence of many witnesses entrust to reliable men who will also be qualified to teach others" (2 Tim. 2:2). Finally, Jesus revealed the full breadth of His duplication plan when He told His disciples, "I tell you the truth, anyone who has faith in Me will do what I have been doing. He will do even greater things than these, because I am going to the Father" (Jn. 14:12).

The Lord's great plan to duplicate Himself in the earth was culminated in the "Great Commission" when He told His disciples, "...go and make disciples of all nations..." (Mt. 28:19). To "make disciples" means to "make students." I believe Jesus would not have left the earth if He had not duplicated Himself in His disciples. In His last days before ascending to Heaven, He probably told those men, "What I put in you Peter, I want you to duplicate in others. What I put in you, John, you must duplicate in others. The same goes for you, James; and for you, Bartholomew. Matthew, I want you to go into the world and duplicate what you are."

The principle of duplication places a solemn responsibility on each of us. We need to examine ourselves from a new perspective. Since the miracle of duplication in your life must begin with you, ask yourself, "What do I need to remove from my life so I can duplicate myself in someone else?" What must you do to duplicate yourself, and are you in a position to get the job done? The men who joined David in the cave of Adullam were not ready to duplicate anything but failure in others. They had three conditions holding them back. They were in distress, they were in debt, and they were discontented. David had to work this stuff out of them so they could duplicate.

David must have done something right, because he started with only 400 men, but he wound up with all of Israel coming under him in unity! What happened? David's followers duplicated themselves, and the people they influenced also duplicated themselves. In the end, thousands of dedicated and unified people were devoting their strength and effort to make David king because they had perceived the purpose and will of God.

God Selects What Man Rejects

Isn't it good to know that when you are passed over, when people count you insignificant, when people pass by you to flock around the stars of the hour, God knows what He has placed in you? You may be standing there, knowing you have the same level of anointing and potential in you as the one the crowds adore. Perhaps you have been rejected because you don't have a certain look, tone of voice, or an ear-tickling message. Isn't it good to know that even though man rejects you, God has accepted, elected, and selected you? Take heart, child of God. You are elected by God. He declares that you are going to be all that you are supposed to be in this life, and you are going to bring glory to His name. It is your destiny.

The Bible says all of God's ways are excellent (see Ps. 150:2). Now God is calling us to walk in excellence like our Master. We need to realize that true excellence transforms mere "good" into an enemy of "better" and "best." Have you ever said to yourself, "Well, this is good enough"? (I have.) Good becomes an enemy of better whenever you could have done better, but you said, "This is good enough." When you could have reached for the best, but instead you said, "This is good enough." God is bringing us into a place of excellence where "good" is not good enough. Don't stop until your "good" gets better and your "better" becomes best.

Psalm 139:14a declares, "I praise You because I am fearfully and wonderfully made." I personalize this verse and declare God's truth about myself: "According to this Scripture, I am somebody special!" Another important thing to remember is that nobody is an island. We belong to a body with many members. You are not an island, you are part of a great "continent of God."

You will never fulfill your destiny alone. Just as He ordains that little babies be reared by parents until adulthood, He also uses others to mentor you into your destiny. If this is new to you, then think about Moses, Joshua, Samuel, Esther, Solomon, Elisha, the 12 disciples, Paul, Timothy, John Mark and Titus. Where would they have been without the mentors God gave them?

There never was an Elisha until there was an Elijah. Frankly, I believe there was a mentor somewhere in Elijah's life, although it might not be mentioned in Scripture. There never was a Joshua until there was a Moses. Even Moses was mentored for 40 years in the house of Pharaoh, where he received a classic education and learned the customs of the Egyptians in the palace. Yet God still wasn't finished with him. After Moses made a rash mistake, God took him to the back side of a mountain and put him under a man named Jethro, whose name literally means "excellence." God used Jethro to impart the spirit of excellence to Moses.

For another 40 years, Moses humbly submitted to and served Jethro, and received the spirit of excellence. He taught Moses how to do things in an excellent way by defeating "good" and "better" and only settling for "the best" for God. God used Jethro to impart excellence to Moses so that when he became the leader of Israel at the age of 80, he could do it with excellence. Nothing was half done. Whatever he did, he did in an excellent way. No wonder Pharaoh had to say, "Take them Moses. Get on out of here." He couldn't resist Moses because he was dealing with an excellent God.

Since we are dealing with an excellent God, the things we do for God must be done in an excellent way. This standard of excellence has been "rejected by man but selected by God"! Some people will protest when you insist on excellence for God. They will say, "It doesn't take all of that. You have to stay within a certain budget and do it this way." This kind of attitude produces only "second-best" things for God. Why do we try to give God something that is second-best when God is excellent? When we come to the place and realize that God is excellent, then we will begin to understand that we have been *selected* by an *excellent God!*

The God of excellence says in His Word that I am fearfully and wonderfully made. My mama and daddy didn't make me. Their chromosomes came together to help produce my outward appearance, but my spirit, the real me, comes directly from the God of excellence. I was made in His image and likeness. God fashioned me.

For You created my inmost being; You knit me together in my mother's womb. I praise You because I am fearfully and wonderfully made; Your works are wonderful, I know that full well. My frame was not hidden from You when I was made in the secret place. When I was woven together in the depths of the earth, Your eyes saw my unformed body. All the days ordained for me were written in Your book before one of them came to be (Psalm 139:13-16).

David said of the Lord:

O Lord, You have searched me and You know me. You know when I sit and when I rise; You perceive my thoughts from afar. You discern my going out and my lying down; You are familiar with all my ways. Before a word is on my tongue You know it completely, O Lord. ... if I make my bed in the depths [sheol]*, You are there. If I rise on the wings of the dawn, if I settle on the far side of the sea, even there Your hand will guide me, Your right hand will hold me fast* (Psalm 139:1-4;8b-10).

It should be clear that you are somebody special—no matter what man thinks about you. You have to understand this if you want to accomplish "great exploits" for God like Joshua. Joshua approached an impossible task after his mentor's death, equipped only with the word of the Lord about his situation: "Be strong and courageous, because you will lead these people to inherit the land... . Have I not commanded you? Be strong and courageous. Do not be terrified; do not be discouraged, for the Lord your God will be with you wherever you go" (Josh. 1:6,9). As it turned out, God's word and presence were more than enough for the task.

Man says, "Well, you don't speak very well, so I reject you." Moses stuttered, but he obeyed God and triumphed over it (see Ex. 4:10, Lev. 23:44). Man says, "You are not the type of person I want to hang around with, so I reject you." Timothy, the "half-Jewish, half-Greek" disciple of Paul faced this prejudice and triumphed in spite of it (see Acts 16:1-4). Man says, "You are a religious fanatic, so I reject you." Paul was ridiculed by the Athenian philosophers at first, but he met them face to face at the Areopagus and ultimately won many disciples for Christ (see Acts 17:18-34). People will take every opportunity they can get to reject you because they feel it makes them somehow superior. Frankly, I am glad that man had nothing to do with my selection. I was selected by God, and that seals the matter. Remember: No matter what man thinks about you, you are fearfully made.

I don't know about your experience, but I never thought I was "wonderfully made" or "terrific" until I began to study God's Word to find out what He had to say about me. Once I began to discover the truth about myself, I began to stand up on the inside. I no longer needed the opinions of others to understand who I was—my Maker had settled the matter. People will cut you up and slander you with their mouth, but despite all of the mindless chatter and empty talk of men, God says that I am fearfully and wonderfully made. Why listen to empty noise when you can hear the wonderful words of God?

Now I can look at people who reject me and declare, "I might not look or act like you, but I am terrific and tremendous!" I am amazed at God's divine ability to make all of us different yet individually "terrific and tremendous." When God says I am wonderfully made, it means I am amazing and miraculous. Never forget that though every man be a liar, God's Word about you is true (see Rom. 3:4)!

If you ever doubt God's Word about your unique qualities and miraculous creation, consider how you arrived on this planet. You are a walking miracle that survived when the odds were literally 300 million-to-one against it! When your parents came together, of the millions of sperm released, only one (in most cases) survived the journey and battle to reach the egg and fertilize it. You had one chance in 300 million of getting here—but you did it. I don't know how you feel about it, but I say, "Well, it was a miracle that I even got here. Since I'm here, I'm going to show the world that I'm miraculous!"

I remember a story told by the late Dr. Martin Luther King about some scientists who wanted to define the physical worth of the human body. They conducted chemical analysis on the human body to measure and quantify all the elements such as iron, zinc, copper, calcium, magnesium, etc. In the end, they totalled up everything left after the water content was removed, and calculated the total worth of the human body to be a grand total of 98 cents at that time!

That makes you feel glad to be human, doesn't it? Scientists say the total net worth of your body is only 98 cents (I think the value has risen well above a dollar due to inflation). You can get more than that for a bag of empty aluminum cans! I think Dr. King followed that story with questions like: "How can you put a value on a living man? How can you say a man like William Shakespeare the playwright, with all of his genius and literary artistry, is only worth 98 cents? How can you say a man like Abraham Lincoln or George Washington Carver is only worth 98 cents? Was Jesus Christ, whose body hung on a cross for you and me, worth only 98 cents?"

The total value of the chemicals and materials in the human body may only add up to a little over a dollar today, but the body of a man is only his house. The essence of his being is found in his spirit, that part of his makeup that bears the image and likeness of his Creator. I remember Dr. King driving home his point by noting that the greatest treasure in the earth is not found in the diamond mines of Africa, or in the oil fields of the Middle East; it is found in the graveyards of the world, where millions of people were buried with their dreams unfulfilled, and their visions untapped.

You don't have to join the ranks of the unfulfilled. You may have been rejected by men, but you were selected by God! Don't allow what God has planted in you to be driven out of you. Don't allow yourself to be buried with your dreams and visions. They are a treasure that nobody can recover or retrieve once you are gone. When the devil tries to get you down by telling you that you are going to fail because your bills are behind, just say, "I'm awesome. I have a way of pulling myself out of this condition." When dark clouds seem to hang over your life for a lifetime, when you wonder if it will always be "raining" in your life, tell your adversary, "I'm awesome because God says so."

Take heart. God has given you the ability to weather the storm. Yes, you may sway from side to side, but God will not allow you to roll over. You might bend, but you won't break. Release the Word of God within you. Speak it out when the devil comes around and tell him the truth as God declares it: "I'm awesome!" Of course the devil already knows that you are awesome...that is why he so persistently tries to tear you down and keep you from grasping the truth about yourself. The Bible says:

> ...*God opposes the proud but gives grace to the humble. Submit yourselves, then, to God. Resist the devil, and he will flee from you* (James 4:6-7).

The Greek word translated as "flee" in this verse literally means the devil is going to tuck his tail between his legs and run! Tell the devil, "God says I'm awesome! Not only am I awesome, but I'm incredible! If you hem me in so I can't get out the door, I'll climb out through the window. If you back me into a corner and brag that

I can't climb out of the window or go through the door, then I'll go through the roof!"

A few days later, when Jesus again entered Capernaum, the people heard that He had come home. So many gathered that there was no room left, not even outside the door, and He preached the word to them. Some men came, bringing to Him a paralytic, carried by four of them. Since they could not get him to Jesus because of the crowd, they made an opening in the roof above Jesus and, after digging through it, lowered the mat the paralyzed man was lying on. When Jesus saw their faith, He said to the paralytic, "Son, your sins are forgiven" (Mark 2:1-5).

What about the men who couldn't get through the crowds to bring their paralyzed friend to Jesus? Did they give up? No, they came through the roof! They lowered their friend down to the Healer because they were incredible people who refused to allow the devil to stop them. You have to realize that you are incredible because God made you that way. You can do anything that you want to do.

God has made us great and awesome. I was flying home from Chicago thinking, "This plane holds over 300 people. Man built this thing with tons of steel and loaded it with all these people, yet it defies gravity! Every time this big airplane rolls down the runway and lifts off, it winks at gravity and says, 'I beat you again.' " The incredible mind of man didn't stop there. We sent astronauts to the moon a number of years ago, and I heard their spacecraft reached a speed of over 30,000 miles an hour! Those men circled the moon while taking close-up photographs, and then they actually landed on the moon and went for an extended hike while all the world watched on live television! Somehow, scientists and engineers had packed in enough fuel for them to reach the moon, circle it, land, lift off again, circle it again while taking more pictures, and then come home again! Isn't that incredible? Man, in all of his intelligence, even designed that spacecraft to pass safely through the different layers of earth's atmosphere, even though the outer hull heats up to some 2000 or 3000 degrees! That would incinerate any normal aircraft, but man designed that special space vehicle to pass through that inferno while keeping its human cargo alive and well.

If such a small and limited creature like man can walk on the moon's surface, what do you think about God the unlimited Creator? We are incredible, fabulous, and exceptional only because God made us in His own image. Now the devil, the enemy of your soul, is the most skillful accuser in the universe. He will tell you, "You think too much of yourself." Don't accept his lies. You need to let him know, "No, I do not. I am only repeating what I have heard my Father in Heaven say! This is what God says about me in His Word!" Once you really realize that you were *created* a fabulous, incredible, awesome, miraculous, amazing, and exceptional person, then you are going to do something fabulous, incredible, awesome, miraculous, amazing, and exceptional!

Now who wouldn't want to duplicate all this in somebody else? If you really are extraordinary, exceptional, fabulous, and miraculous, wouldn't you want somebody else to be like you? Why do you think God put a core in the apple? Why did He put a seed at the heart of the peach and cherry? What is in the middle of a plum? What is in the middle of an orange? (I'm not talking about the sterile "seedless" versions cooked up by man as a genetic "improvement.") God designed these fruits this way so they could *reproduce themselves* once they had fulfilled their purpose as a source of food and refreshment for man and the animal kingdom!

From the beginning, God commanded the natural realm, and Adam in particular, to reproduce and multiply (see Gen. 1:11,28). This mandate continued after the Flood when God commanded Noah and his sons to "multiply" and subdue the earth (see Gen. 9:1). What is reproduction? It is duplication. God is saying to us, "I want you to duplicate; therefore, so I put a seed in you so you could duplicate yourself." He didn't want the earth to be without your kind, so He designed you with natural seed (or the human reproduction process) so you could duplicate yourself. Since you are more than mere flesh, God made special provision for your eternal nature.

"For you have been born again, not of perishable seed, but of imperishable, through the living and enduring word of God" (1 Pet. 1:23). God doesn't want us to be satisfied simply with physical reproduction. He gave us *new seed* through His own bloodline in Jesus Christ, so we could duplicate the *Christ in us* within the lives of our children and others the Lord brings into our lives! Jesus did not leave the earth until He had duplicated Himself in at least 12 people (at least 120 people had been so affected by His life that they obediently waited for His gift in the Upper Room). The 12 disciples (Judas Iscariot was replaced) and those in the Upper Room turned the world upside down within one generation by preaching Christ!

Jesus Christ must have done a thorough job in duplicating Himself. You and I need to do the same. I pray that as you read this book, the things God has spoken to my heart will be duplicated in you. When you have put them into practice and tested them along with the other things you have learned, then you in turn will duplicate yourself in somebody else. In the end, God's Word will again turn the world upside down! You are not to leave this earth before you have duplicated yourself. You should make a commitment to God and say, "I'm not going anywhere until I duplicate myself in a hundred people. I don't care if I have to live to be a hundred, please don't take me off this earth until I duplicate myself and plant myself in at least a hundred people. When I leave here, I want to see the holy things you have planted in me live on in the lives of at least a hundred people."

If you duplicate yourself in a hundred people, and if those hundred people duplicate themselves in other people, just think how great the Kingdom of God will become. The fact is that it has to start in a place like your home, your church, and your heart. It has to start in a cave like Adullam, or in backwater towns like Bethlehem and Capernaum. God's Word says, "Who despises the day of small things?" (Zech. 4:10a) It has to start in a cave, a womb of adversity, or a valley of decision. This is the way everybody starts, but when it is all said and done, you will reproduce and your fruit will spread abroad.

There are some practical things you and I can to do increase our fruitfulness. We all have some things we need to build into our character, and some things we need to remove. Some of the things we must allow the Spirit of God to plant in us include:

Self-worth. Many men and women have no idea how much they are worth, and the devil isn't going to tell them. The truth is that you are worth more than you think you are! King Solomon spent over $300,000,000,000 to build a temple "to house God's glory." The Bible plainly states that *we* are the temple of the Holy Ghost (see 1 Cor. 3:17; 6:19), so we are at least worth the amount Solomon spent to build his temple! We cannot grasp the value represented by that figure because we have never seen that much money.

We might have seen a $1,000, $10,000, or even a $100,000, but when we say $300 billion dollars our minds have to reach out to grasp its meaning. Consider this: If two, three, or nine believers sit together in one room, and each one is worth at least the cost of Solomon's temple, then their combined "value" exceeds billions and billions of dollars!

When the devil looks at us, he understands our worth. He fumes because he understands how valuable we are to the Creator he rebelled against. He also knows we *don't* understand our worth in the sight of God. Jesus said that when one sinner gets saved, all of Heaven rejoices over that one even *more* than the "ninety-nine sheep" already in the fold! (See Matthew 18:12-13.) If you have a powerful calculator, then multiply 300 billion (the cost of Solomon's temple) by 99. If your calculator can hold that large of a sum, then understand that this is just a glimpse of the "worth" of each sinner who gives his heart to Jesus! We need to build this understanding of our worth and value into our character.

When the devil says you are nothing, let him know that you will never be nothing, your mama wasn't nothing, and your daddy wasn't nothing. Instead tell him, "I'm something." You have to talk back to him because if you don't, he'll cut you up with his own words. You have to tell him, "I'm worth something and I know I'm worth something!"

Self-confidence. Paul the apostle wrote to the Philippians: "Being confident of this, that He who began a good work in you will carry it on to completion until the day of Christ Jesus" (Phil. 1:6). I love that Scripture verse because, as I said earlier, I'm miraculous just by the very fact that I'm here! God started a good work in me, and He is not a God who starts something and doesn't finish it. If He started it, He is going to finish it. Any way you want to look at it, I've got a bright future! I have hope for tomorrow because I know that He is going to finish what He started in me. The devil knows it too.

Once we grasp the fact that God Himself is going to complete His work in us, then we will put the devil under our feet and keep him there! Today, I am confident that God is going to do it. You can say anything you want to say, but I have confidence that what God started in me, He is going to complete in me. One writer wrote, "I might not sing like angels and preach like Paul, but I want you to know one thing, I'm confident that what He started in me He's going to complete and finish."

I don't know what God started in you, but I know He started something. If He didn't, you wouldn't be here. It doesn't matter where you are today. He started something in me too, and I am what I am today by the design of God. I am confident He will get me where I need to be tomorrow. The men who sit with David in the cave of Adullam today will get to sit with him in the king's palace tomorrow. David planted himself in them, and he declared how he wanted his kingdom run. "This is how I want the gold dispersed. This is how I want warfare to take place."

David poured himself into them so that when he took them out of the cave, he had a seasoned and disciplined administrative staff and fighting force. Every member of his 400-man force could throw a stone with his left hand as well as his right with deadly accuracy. His army could go out against nations and come back alive because they were confident, disciplined, and trained by David himself. I dare you to become confident. When the devil calls your confidence "pride," just tell him, "No, I'm not prideful. I'm just confident in my God, the Creator who planted this ability within me and began a good work in my life! I'm not cocky; I'm just confident in the ability God gave me!"

If you think you can't do it, then a lot of the people you influence will duplicate that weakness in themselves. You won't pour good things from yourself into others because you feel you can't do it. You need to have confidence that you can do it because you have been "called" to do it.

Self-motivation. A self-motivated person is a self-starter with initiative, a hustler, someone who gets things started and finishes them. A self-starter is someone who doesn't need anyone to "light his fire" because his fire is already burning! I am a self-starter because I am motivated by the very fact that I'm here. I am motivated by the fact that I am fearfully and wonderfully made. I don't need anybody to push me out of bed each morning—I jump out of bed!

I don't let the day rule me; I take control of my day and I handle it because I know God made this day for me. I decide that I'm going to handle this day because "this is the day that the Lord has made" and I will rejoice and be glad in it! (See Psalm 118:24.) I'm not going to be sad, downtrodden, or defeated today. I am going to be happy and blessed today. I'm going to take control of this day and do the miraculous because through Christ I am a self-starter.

Self-improvement. Don't ever get stagnant. The same apostle who said he had learned to be "content" in every circumstance also declared, "I can do everything through Him who gives me strength" (see Phil. 4:11-13). He also described his continual drive for greater godliness and productivity when he wrote, "But one thing I do: Forgetting what is behind and straining toward what is ahead, I press on toward the goal to win the prize for which God has called me heavenward in Christ Jesus" (Phil. 3:13b-14).

I heard one Bible teacher say that when the Bible says, "Study to shew thyself approved unto God, a workman that needeth not to be ashamed, rightly dividing the word of truth" (2 Tim. 2:15 KJV), it has a different meaning than what most of us believe. He claimed that the word translated as *study* means "to get educated" so you might have a higher opinion of God. If you are ignorant and unlearned in your understanding of God and His Word, then you might believe He is a God of poverty. As you come into the knowledge of God, you quickly see that God can bring you above poverty. His Word paints a picture of God putting a ring on your finger, a robe on your back, and a chain around your neck. As you learn what God *says* He wants you to have and become, then your opinion of God is lifted to a new mentality and a new level.

You should strive in Christ to be the best you can possibly be. Don't try to bring God down to your level; instead tell people that God is the Healer. Tell them God provides for you because His name is Jehovah-Jireh. Tell them that when your life was like a raging sea tossed to and fro, when your mind was just about to give out, Jehovah-Shalom stepped in and gave you peace. Tell them He is a Peacemaker because you've come into the *knowledge* that He has become your peace.

Self-sacrifice. People in the "me" generation have a lot of trouble with "self-sacrifice." Nevertheless, we can only duplicate ourselves by denying self for the Lord and the good of others. Whenever an opportunity to do good to others presents itself, we should do it, even though it is a sacrifice. Paul wrote, "I beseech you therefore, brethren, by the mercies of God, that ye present your bodies a living sacrifice, holy, acceptable unto God, which is your reasonable service" (Rom. 12:1 KJV).

Many of God's people avoid this "living sacrifice" message because of the "sacrifice" word. The problem with "living" sacrifices is that they have a tendency to sometimes crawl off the altar! The Bible is clear; it leaves us with no choice. It says, "present your bodies a living sacrifice." As long as you're living, stay on the altar and let God use you. Stay on the altar and be that sacrifice. Although you sometimes are required to become a sacrifice for others, you must realize that others are being blessed by what you sacrifice and what you do.

The only way to live is to die. The only way to grow is to give yourself away. You have to be a sacrifice and give yourself. This is why Paul said, "And I will very gladly spend and be spent for you; though the more abundantly I love you, the less I be loved" (2 Cor. 12:15 KJV). This verse is fine to quote, but is it in your character? Will you "be spent" for others? Giving and self-sacrifice must become a part of us if we want to duplicate ourselves.

Self-control. Can you keep your balance and maintain dignity, or are there areas in your life that are *out of control*?

Self-determination. You must be determined. Don't quit; be determined to accomplish, to achieve, to overcome, and to finish what you started. Go to bed thinking about your calling, and wake up thinking about it. Trust the Christ within you and declare, "I can do it." Develop a holy "I can do" attitude, and avoid the "I can't do" atmosphere. Gravity says man can't fly. Gravity says that nothing that is heavier than air can fly. Man said, "I can too!" It took centuries of dreams, sketches, failures, and experiments, but man did what he dreamed he could do.

Paul told the Philippians, "I can do all things through Christ which strengtheneth me" (Phil. 4:13 KJV). You can do it. Be determined and know that you can. "For as [a man] thinketh in his heart, so is he" (Prov. 23:7a KJV). Think on and declare the incredible things God says about you!

Chapter 5

Another Turn on the Potter's Wheel

ave you ever known people you just love to be around because they were impressive, even when they don't say anything? Somehow they are impressive just because of who they are and because of their God-given personalities. Many of these people can be good leaders, but they still need some "character work." They may be anointed and they may have good leadership abilities, but they have some character weaknesses that are obvious to all those who know them.

This is what Jesus was referring to when He told Peter:

> *Simon, Simon, Satan has asked to sift you as wheat. But I have prayed for you, Simon, that your faith may not fail. And when you have turned back, strengthen your brothers* (Luke 22:31-32).

There is no doubt that Peter was anointed, or that he was the first of the 12 disciples to receive the revelation that Christ Jesus was the Son of the living God. Jesus said Peter's dramatic revelation came directly from His Father in Heaven (see Mt. 16:16-17). Peter had the revelation and he was anointed, but Peter also needed some serious character work! When Jesus stood before Caiaphas, the high priest, Peter was in the courtyard outside, denying his Lord with a string of curses for emphasis (see Mt. 26:74-75).

Peter's character flaws, particularly his fear of men, followed him throughout his ministry. On the one hand, Peter the anointed apostle was so powerful that whenever his shadow fell on the sick, the diseased, or the demon-possessed, they were instantly delivered and healed, and they rose from their beds! Yet that same man, Peter the apostle, was rebuked publicly by the apostle Paul in Galatia because he suddenly stopped associating with non-Jewish believers the moment Jewish believers from Jerusalem showed up!

> *But when Peter was come to Antioch, I withstood him to the face, because he was to be blamed. For before that certain came from James, he did eat with the Gentiles: but when they were come, he withdrew and separated himself, fearing them which were of the circumcision. And the other Jews dissembled likewise with him; insomuch that Barnabas also was carried away with their dissimulation* (Galatians 2:11-13 KJV).

Paul warned Peter that if circumcision or salvation came through the law as his actions implied, then Christ died in vain! Peter obviously had a character problem that tended to surface at the worst of times. Does this sound familiar? Some of the most anointed people around us can be doing some of the greatest things in our generation—even while their own character is still under development. Nobody has "arrived" at perfection.

In addition to the "character flaws" all of us do our best to conceal, we have another obstacle attempting to block our path to perfection in Christ. He is the adversary of our souls, the evil rebel who is out to defeat us and thwart the progress of God's people. The devil knows that we are incredible, but he also knows about our weaknesses. One of the best ways to defeat his work in your life is to consider the devil's track record and learn from it.

Never underestimate your opponents in any endeavor, and especially your chief opponent, the devil. He has already brought down the prettiest! He stole handsome Absalom's heart and led him to plot the murder of his own father! (See Second Samuel 14:25; 15:4-14.) The devil temporarily swayed the man whom God called "a man after My own heart" (Acts 13:22) when he caused David to fall into sin with Bathsheba (see 2 Sam. 11), and again when he enticed David to disobey God and number Israel (see 2 Sam. 24:10). The devil deceived and ensnared Solomon, God's wisest, with the affections of foreign women (see 1 Kings 11:4). He ensnared Samson, God's strongest, with the comforting arms of Delilah (see Judg. 16:13-17). The devil caused the prophets Elijah and Jonah to doubt, run, and hide (see 1 Kings 19:2-4; Jon. 1:3). In fact, somewhere in time, the devil had led all of them to follow his lead instead of the will of God.

What about you? Are you prepared for the devil's fiery darts and evil devices? He is aiming at you, but you are *not defenseless*! You have the same weapons the apostle Paul described in his letter to the Corinthians:

> *For though we live in the world, we do not wage war as the world does. The weapons we fight with are not the weapons of the world. On the contrary, they have divine power to demolish strongholds. We demolish arguments and every pretension that sets itself up against the knowledge of God, and we take captive every thought to make it obedient to Christ* (2 Corinthians 10:3-5).

We need to start some spiritual "SWAT" teams to conduct spiritual warfare on behalf of the saints and the Church! We need it. The devil is out to shape human personalities after his own twisted image of rebellion, selfishness, and unholiness. He is shooting his fiery darts at us now, but we've got to stand with the whole armor of God (see Eph. 6:10-18). By "personality," I am referring to the quality or fact of being a *particular* and unique person. The only image we are designed to imitate is the infinite and holy image of our Creator.

Potter's Wheel

God knows how to raise up those "voted the most unlikely to succeed in life." He loves to find the people most of us look down on so He can raise them up. He will find you and pick you up out of the field where other people have abandoned you. His restoration process usually includes adversity that is often confused with the attacks of the enemy. There is a clear difference in motive and method between the two. God gave the prophet Jeremiah a beautiful illustration of His restoration process for broken and flawed men:

> *This is the word that came to Jeremiah from the Lord: "Go down to the potter's house, and there I will give you My message." So I went down to the potter's house, and I saw him working at the wheel. But the pot he was shaping from the clay was marred in his hands; so the potter formed it into another pot, shaping it as seemed best to him* (Jeremiah 18:1-4).

I really like the fact that Jeremiah saw a work in the potter's hand that was *marred*. Did you notice the next part of the Scripture? It basically says, "I know it's marred. So?" God makes each marred pot in His Kingdom into "another pot" by reshaping it as it seems best to Him. I don't know about you, but that is a comforting picture for *this* "marred pot."

I don't know what you're going through, but I know God has a plan or a "man" to pick you up and straighten you out where you are crooked or marred. If you are still on the Potter's wheel, if God is in the middle of reshaping an area of your life from what you were to what He wants you to be, then many people are going to misunderstand you! The King James Version of the Bible says the potter worked the marred clay pot on the pottery wheel and "made it again another vessel" (Jer. 18:4). Don't be surprised when you are misunderstood during that difficult and embarrassing stage between "it and another." You are still a marred pot, but God is making you into another! What do you say and how to you think of yourself when you are between "it and another"? I believe the right response is: "So?"

That word separates our flawed state from "another" shape in the Master's mind. You are being broken and remolded in front of the world as you take "another" shape in the Master Potter's hands. Like Paul, we should glory in our weaknesses because in them, God's strength is made visible in our lives! Paul declared:

> *But He said to me, "My grace is sufficient for you, for My power is made perfect in weakness." Therefore I will boast all the more gladly about my weaknesses, so that Christ's power may rest on me. That is why, for Christ's sake, I delight in weaknesses, in insults, in hardships, in persecutions, in difficulties. For when I am weak, then I am strong* (2 Corinthians 12:9-10).

This doesn't mean we should make excuses for our weaknesses or failures—it means we must lean on the powerful arm of God to *change* us in another form as it pleases Him. When people don't like you because you are "marred" right now, then just tell those people, "So? I'm on the Potter's wheel. I am right where I am supposed to be—in His hands. He is making me into *another!*" When people look down their nose at you because you are "marred" in their eyes, and you know God hasn't completed your transformation to "another," just tell them, "So? I am being reshaped into *another!*"

Your friends and critics may see all your downfalls and shortcomings, and eagerly rehearse your failures to you at every opportunity. Just tell them in love, "So? This is what God says about me. He knows I am marred in His hands, but He says, 'So?' " Remember how you landed on the Master Potter's wheel. Remember who put you there, and why! Jesus knew you and I had flaws, failures, and mistakes when the Father asked Him to redeem us with His blood. Do you know what He had to say about us? He said, "So? I know they have been rejected, stepped on, dropped, and bent, but they are Mine and I will redeem them with My own life."

When other people don't understand your worth or your value this week, just look at them and say, "So? I'm on my way to becoming *another.* I might not be what you want me to be right now, but just wait until I come off of this potter's wheel! I might not be in the place you want me to be right now because I'm marred, but all I really needed was for somebody to pick me up and invest his time in me. I needed someone to take the time and effort to straighten me out and make me fit for the Master's use. I know I am marred, even in the hands of the Potter, but God says, 'So?' "

"Pruning" is a natural part of our life in the hands of God. Considering how often Jesus talked about our perfection in God's hands, it is amazing that people are so quick to judge and so slow to acknowledge the work of God in the lives of individuals! Jesus described our remolding and remaking process in His parable of the vine and the branches in the Gospel of John:

I am the true vine, and My Father is the gardener. He cuts off every branch in Me that bears no fruit, while every branch that does bear fruit He prunes so that it will be even more fruitful. You are already clean because of the word I have spoken to you. Remain in Me, and I will remain in you. No branch can bear fruit by itself; it must remain in the vine. Neither can you bear fruit unless you remain in Me. I am the vine; you are the branches. If a man remains in Me and I in him, he will bear much fruit; apart from Me you can do nothing (John 15:1-5).

There are several things that all of us need to rule out of our personalities and lives. All of these, if they are tolerated or encouraged to grow in our lives, can become a deadly virus or malignant tumor capable of destroying everything good the Lord has done in our lives.

Selfishness is an evil branch that will hinder you at every turn in your life. The only fruit it produces is more of itself. Selfish people are only concerned about their own welfare at the expense or disregard of others. The selfish person says, "I'm only concerned about me, me, me, and especially me." If you want to be successful in God's Kingdom and reach the place of preeminence God has ordained for you, there *appear* to be two ways to get there: You can get there by walking with people or by running over people.

The selfish believer generally wants to take the quick route to success by running over people. He rushes to grasp the outward tokens of success and recognition among men, and then he looks down his nose at others and gloats because they don't have the same outward signs of holiness or prosperity that he possesses. The problem is that there are *never* two ways to fulfill God's plan. There is only *one way*—and that is simply *God's way*, as it is spelled out in His Word and revealed by His Holy Spirit. Jesus bluntly ruled out selfishness and allowed no room for self-justification or excuses:

Then He said to them all: "If anyone would come after Me, he must deny himself and take up his cross daily and follow Me. For whoever wants to save his life will lose it, but whoever loses his life for Me will save it. What good is it for a man to gain the whole world, and yet lose or forfeit his very self?" (Luke 9:23-25)

You must rule selfishness out of your character. It begins with a choice, and is perfected on the Potter's wheel of daily living in Christ.

Self-righteousness is another worthless branch that must be ruled out of our lives. Self-righteousness is the chief fruit of hypocrisy in our lives. It was the most distinguishable and hated characteristic of the Pharisees, the people who ultimately arranged the wrongful crucifixion of Jesus!

*Jesus began to speak first to His disciples, saying, "Be on your guard against the yeast of the Pharisees, which is **hypocrisy**"* (Luke 12:1b).

*Woe to you, teachers of the law and Pharisees, you hypocrites! You clean the outside of the cup and dish, but inside they are full of greed and self-indulgence. Blind Pharisee! First clean the inside of the cup and dish, and then the outside also will be clean. Woe to you, teachers of the law and Pharisees, you hypocrites! You are like whitewashed tombs, which look beautiful on the outside but on the inside are full of dead men's bones and everything unclean. In the same way, **on the outside you appear to people as righteous** but on the inside you are full of hypocrisy and wickedness* (Matthew 23:25-28).

But when he [John the Baptist] *saw many of the Pharisees and Sadducees coming to where he was baptizing, he said to them: "You brood of vipers! Who warned you to flee from the coming wrath? **Produce fruit in keeping with repentance.** And do not think you can say to yourselves, 'We have Abraham as our father.' I tell you that out of these stones God can raise up children for Abraham. The ax is already at the root of the trees, and every tree that does not produce good fruit will be cut down and thrown into the fire"* (Matthew 3:7-10).

The Pharisees elevated themselves above other people by adopting a false standard of holiness based on *outward appearance* and actions while ignoring the true motives of the heart. The only righteousness that God recognizes and receives is the righteousness we receive through His Son, Jesus Christ:

> *But God hath chosen the foolish things of the world to confound the wise; and God hath chosen the weak things of the world to confound the things which are mighty; and base things of the world, and things which are despised, hath God chosen, yea, and things which are not, to bring to nought things that are: that no flesh should glory in His presence. But of Him are ye in Christ Jesus, who of God is made unto us wisdom, and righteousness, and sanctification, and redemption* (1 Corinthians 1:27-30 KJV).

Self-pity is the fruitless branch that encourages you to sit down in despair and say, "Nobody loves me. Nobody cares about me." Self-pity likes to see you have pity parties in your corner. Pity parties always start with *self*. The only other person who enjoys your pitiful pity parties is the devil. He is the only one who shows up with his party hat and whistle to cheer you on into deeper and deeper displays of selfishness and unbelief. God doesn't show up at our pity parties, unless He comes to shut them down. Elijah the prophet discovered this the hard way!

Elijah was the powerful prophet of God who challenged the prophets of Baal to a showdown before the whole nation of Israel. He called down the fire of God and destroyed the altar of Baal, and then killed 850 devilish priests of Baal, turning Israel's heart back to God!

Now Ahab told Jezebel everything Elijah had done and how he had killed all the prophets with the sword. So Jezebel sent a messenger to Elijah to say, "May the gods deal with me, be it ever so severely, if by this time tomorrow I do not make your life like that of one of them." Elijah was afraid and ran for his life. When he came to Beersheba in Judah, he left his servant there, while he himself went a day's journey into the desert. He came to a broom tree, sat down under it and prayed that he might die. "I have had enough, Lord," he said. "Take my life; I am no better than my ancestors" (1 Kings 19:1-4).

Elijah had just single-handedly killed 850 heathen prophets, yet when one woman named Jezebel threatened to kill Elijah, the mighty prophet of God tucked his tail between his legs and ran for his life! When he finally stopped running and sat down, self-pity really set in. He told God, "I just want to die." God doesn't let us get by with self-pity. He sent an angel with a summons for a "40-day counseling appointment" with God at Mount Horeb. Once again the prophet rehearsed his "Poor me" story with God, and added the claim, "...The Israelites have rejected Your covenant, broken down Your altars, and put your prophets to death with the sword. I am the only one left, and now they are trying to kill me too" (1 Kings 19:10). God quickly straightened out Elijah's warped perspective and permanently ended his pity party by telling him there were 7,000 other faithful people whose knees had not bowed down to Baal (see 1 Kings 19:18).

Jonah was another prophet whose pity party is remembered even in our day as an example of wrong behavior that was quickly corrected by God. After his initial disobedience and encounter with the great fish or whale, this reluctant prophet went to Nineveh and preached repentance. When the city heeded his warning and repented, Jonah was upset because he wouldn't get to see them destroyed! He decided to drive his unhappiness home by having a pity party under a gourd bush. God decided to get some amusement out of an unpleasant situation by sending a worm to destroy the gourd bush shielding the pouting prophet's bald head from the heat of the day, giving Jonah a first class sunburn. Jonah was toasted because he insisted on having a pity party when he knew better (see Jon. 4).

Don't have pity parties. Rule self-pity out of your character, because if you pity yourself, you're going to excuse yourself. If you excuse yourself, you will end up trying to make excuses all the way through life. Men may go along with this kind of sham, but God cannot be fooled.

Self-centeredness is a characteristic of little children and immature adults, but it is not an attribute of godliness. Beware if you become concerned only about your own activities or needs. Self-centeredness is a deeper and more deadly problem than selfishness. The selfish person wants to possess and control things for his own benefit, but the self-centered person thinks the universe revolves totally around him and his needs and desires. Satan is self-centered to the extreme, but Jesus is our living demonstration of God's heart:

This is how we know what love is: Jesus Christ laid down His life for us. And we ought to lay down our lives for our brothers. If anyone has material possessions and sees his brother in need but has no pity on him, how can the love of God be in him? Dear children, let us not love with words or tongue but with actions and in truth (1 John 3:16-18).

Self-abuse is another branch of unfruitful human personality that must be removed if we want to prosper in God's Kingdom. Self-abusers treat themselves without compassion and often in a hurtful manner. Most self-abusive behavior stems from self-hatred or extremely low self-esteem. Jesus set the priority for godly self-love when He repeated the second-most important commandment before the Pharisees: "Love your neighbor as yourself" (Mt. 22:39b). The Bible also gives us a solemn warning about abusing our bodies for any reason:

Don't you know that you yourselves are God's temple and that God's Spirit lives in you? If anyone destroys God's temple, God will destroy him; for God's temple is sacred, and you are that temple (1 Corinthians 3:16-17).

You and I are still subject to the natural laws God has established in the earth. I have no business staying up 24 hours today, and then trying to do the same thing the next day for some project or activity. I had better lie down and rest myself—even God rested on the seventh day! Don't abuse yourself spiritually, physically, or emotionally. One of the most important keys to health in these areas is to repent of all sin and fully receive God's forgiveness and grace. This removes the power of guilt or past mistakes from our lives.

Personality is all of the distinctive, individual qualities of a person considered collectively. All of us have individual qualities, although our qualities may seem to match in some cases. It is all those qualities coming together that makes you "you." Only God is wise and powerful enough to make each of us unique, yet also alike in so many ways! The truth is that when He made you, He broke the mold. The closest match to "you" is found in your children, and even there, God gives each child totally unique traits and abilities.

Your son and daughter might look and act like you, but they are not "you." Each personality is created individually distinctive by God. Many times, people can tell a lot about a person by the way he or she dresses, because human beings tend to duplicate what they are on the inside in the way they dress, talk, and act on the outside. A millionaire may dress casually all the time to mislead others, but even casual dress can look either sloppy, or refined and neat.

Money tends to magnify outwardly who we are inside. Money doesn't "make you" great or small, but it can quickly reveal what's hidden behind the wallet or bank account. Nabal, Abigail's husband, was a fool. Although he was wealthy, his money only magnified his foolishness to David. He foolishly judged David to be of no importance and refused to help in David's time of need although David's army had protected Nabal's large herds of livestock from marauders without charge. Only Abigail's gracious spirit saved Nabal from a sudden and violent death, but in the end, God Himself struck Nabal down (see 1 Sam. 25:2-38). If you are a person of quality, money will magnify that quality. Personality, whether good, evil, or "under construction" on the Potter's wheel, is the sum of all of your distinctive, individual qualities. When you step out of your door in the morning, you will make an impression on the people you meet—just because you are you.

You may be taking yet another turn on the Potter's wheel because God is raising you up right now. You might as well get ready for some misunderstanding and adversity because you are between a "stage marred" and "another" stage in God's plan. Paul wrote, "But we all, with open face beholding as in a glass the glory of the Lord, are changed into the same image from glory to glory, even as by the Spirit of the Lord" (2 Cor. 3:18 KJV). God's Spirit is transforming you from "glory to glory," and the transition nearly always leaves some "fleshly" part of you behind because God wants to make you more like Him!

Are you still on the wheel? Tell yourself in the hard times, "I might be marred, but I'm still on the wheel. I might be dysfunctional, but I'm still on the wheel. I might be bent, but I'm still on the wheel. God is making me. God is fixing me. God is restoring me. God is recycling me."

The devil wants you to stop right where you are. He doesn't want you to reach your possibilities. He doesn't want you to discover your potential, let alone reach it! Your solution is simple and direct. Tell that father of liars, "I know where I am because God's Word declares it. I'm going to become 'another' after a while, when my heavenly Father has completed His good work in me. Have you forgotten, devil? Some of the greatest men of God in history were despised, cast down, looked over, and abandoned because they didn't look like much. I'm telling you: Just wait until I come off the wheel of God!"

Chapter 6

The Elect Church of the Selected Rejects

God knows how to pick up rejects. If anybody knows about being a reject, Jesus does. One time I was building a church facility, and I realized that I was a type of a spiritual bricklayer who was helping the Lord "brick His house." I imagined Him looking around the construction site and asking me, "Preacher, what are all these bricks doing laying on the ground?" My habit was to put only the best bricks in the wall. I always threw out the chipped, cracked, and dirty bricks.

I was reminded of one particular building my construction crew had almost finished. As usual, I had thrown out all the chipped, cracked, and dirty bricks, thinking they were unusable for the project. The problem was that when we got down to the end, we didn't have any more "good bricks." I had to send my laborers back to retrieve all of the chipped, broken, and dirty bricks I'd discarded so I could finish the last wall. My natural inspection concluded that because certain bricks were chipped, that I couldn't use them in the wall. If people say that about you, God says, "So? I'm going to use them anyway!" My natural inspection led to my decision that because certain bricks were cracked, I couldn't use them in the wall. If people are saying that about you, God says, "So? What you have rejected I have selected!"

God says His Church will not be complete until you take your place in the wall as He has ordained from eternity! I had to send my laborers to get all the chipped, cracked, and dirty bricks, and I put them in the wall to complete that one project. Do you know what? It didn't look bad at all! This gives us another picture of what the Scriptures mean when they declare, "The stone the builders rejected has become the capstone [or cornerstone]" (Lk. 20:17b). If anybody knows about being rejected, Jesus does.

You might be "cracked," but I'm telling you that God won't consider His Church complete until you are put in your place of destiny in His House, the Church. I know you were marred in the hands of the Potter, but God says, "So?" Most of us assume we can recognize the things God likes or doesn't like. The truth is that we miss it much of the time because we are preoccupied with outward appearances and our impure motives. Many times, the things we approve and choose are not the things God likes! There was a man in the Bible whose father didn't even invite him to his own anointing service because he didn't seem to meet the requirements!

His name was David. Do you sometimes feel like you have not even been invited to your own anointing service?

God told Samuel the prophet to stop mourning for Saul because He had rejected him as king of Israel. Samuel needed to stop mourning over the rejected of God and start anointing the selected of God! (Remember that there is a big difference between what *God* rejects and what *man* rejects.) God commanded Samuel to fill his horn with oil and prepare to anoint a new man as king of Israel (see 1 Sam. 16:1). Even the anointing horn required a blood sacrifice. Some innocent animal gave its life so its horns could contain and pour out the oil that anointed God's chosen. This is a type and shadow of Jesus Christ, the sacrificed Lamb of God, who willingly gave His life so we could live and not die, so we could be selected instead of rejected, so we could be anointed by God for holy service! The only reason you and I are anointed is because the Lamb of God is worthy.

When Samuel went to Bethlehem, he clearly told the elders, along with Jesse, "Consecrate yourselves and come to the sacrifice with me" (1 Sam. 16:5b). Yet in verse 11, Samuel had to ask a question that seems out of place. The Scriptures tell the story:

When they [Jesse's sons] *arrived, Samuel saw Eliab and thought, "Surely the Lord's anointed stands here before the Lord." But the Lord said to Samuel, "Do not consider his appearance or his height, for I have rejected him. The Lord does not look at the things man looks at. Man looks at the outward appearance, but the Lord looks at the heart." ... Jesse had seven of his sons pass before Samuel, but Samuel said to him, "The Lord has not chosen these." So he asked Jesse, "Are these all the sons you have?"* (1 Samuel 16:6-7;10-11).

Although David (whose name means "beloved") was invited to the sacrifice, his father and brothers thought he was too insignificant and unimportant to attend such an important event. Have you ever been overlooked? Take heart. God chooses the people men despise and count insignificant and unimportant. Maybe you were voted the "least likely to succeed in life" by your peers in school. According to the Word of God, you just might rise up and become the most successful member of your class because God has His hand on you!

But God hath chosen the foolish things of the world to confound the wise; and God hath chosen the weak things of the world to confound the things which are mighty; and base things of the world, and things which are despised, hath God chosen, yea, and things which are not, to bring to nought things that are: that no flesh should glory in His presence (1 Corinthians 1:27-29 KJV).

"Samuel, I know that you are looking at the first-born, Eliab, but he's not the one. I know he has big muscles. I know he's the firstborn and he has the right to the inheritance of the firstborn, but he's not the one,

Samuel. The one that I want you to anoint isn't even here yet!"

Jesse had seven of his sons pass before Samuel, but Samuel said to him, "The Lord has not chosen these." So he asked Jesse, "Are these all the sons you have?" "There is still the youngest," Jesse answered, "but he is tending the sheep." Samuel said, "Send for him; we will not sit down until he arrives." So he sent and had him brought in. He was ruddy, with a fine appearance and handsome features. Then the Lord said, "Rise and anoint him; he is the one." So Samuel took the horn of oil and anointed him in the presence of his brothers, and from that day on the Spirit of the Lord came upon David in power..." (1 Samuel 16:10-13).

Samuel the prophet isn't the only one who looks at the outward appearance. Most of us are guilty of this. God gives Samuel an important lesson that we need to learn as well: Don't look on a person's outward countenance, look at the inward man. God told Jeremiah:

The heart is deceitful above all things and beyond cure. Who can understand it? "I the Lord search the heart and examine the mind, to reward a man according to his conduct, according to what his deeds deserve" (Jeremiah 17:9-10).

God is the only one who can clearly see man's heart. A surgeon can expose a man's physical heart and examine it with his eyes and hands, but he can't see the wickedness that is in it. He can see the heart of flesh, but only God can accurately see the wickedness in the heart. This discernment of God is the key factor in His selection of men and women.

Consider the selection patterns of God in the Bible. Cain was Adam's firstborn son, the first man-child born on the earth—but God chose Abel. Ishmael was Abraham's firstborn son—but God chose Isaac. Esau was Isaac's firstborn son, but God chose Jacob. Reuben was Jacob's firstborn son, but God chose Joseph, his youngest. God spoke through Jacob to tell Reuben he was as unstable as water. Manasseh was Joseph's firstborn son, but God chose Ephraim. Eliab was Jesse's firstborn son, but God chose David. Egypt and Babylon were established long before Israel, but God chose Israel.

It doesn't matter when you come, and it doesn't matter how you come, just as long as you come! If you can just get there, if you can put your feet in the world, you're going to be awesome! Well, since you're here, you might as well be awesome. Since you're here and your feet are planted on the earth, you might as well be incredible and extraordinary. Let others talk about you if they want to, but they can't "talk away" what you are, because you are what you are by the grace of God!

Now is the Scripture coming to pass that declares the "...first shall be last; and the last shall be first" (Mt. 19:30 KJV)! This is the day and the generation in which the Lord is using those who come from "beneath and behind." Our generation is like David, the man named "beloved." He was the eighth son, which signifies a *new beginning*. Thank You, Lord God, for choosing us to bring about a new beginning. You and I were chosen to bring about a new beginning in our generation!

Judah had twin sons born of Tamar. The Bible says the midwife saw a hand emerge first, so she tied a red cord around his wrist, assuming he would be the first born. Then the arm went back into the birth canal, and the other baby was born first! This other baby was literally named "Breech" or *Pharez,* because he was born hind-end first. But I want you to know *I'm coming out any way I can*! All I need to do is put my feet on the ground. I'm coming out of this thing! If you are in a valley and the devil wants to keep you there, you need to take a stand in Christ and tell the devil, "If I come out back side first, head first, arm first, or foot first, I'm coming out of here! I may be rejected by man, but I'm selected by God!"

According to the traditions of men and the outward inspection of man's eyes, when the firstborn steps up, man says, "Surely the Lord's anointed stands before me." Samuel the prophet learned something that has been passed down to us: God doesn't see like man sees. I'm telling you that we have come to the point in the latter part of this century when the "last" is coming to the forefront and becoming "first."

You may have been last in a lot of things, but God is bringing you to the forefront. People may have talked about you and listed all of the things you "couldn't do," but God has raised you up to bring you to the forefront. Now people will begin to say, "What do you think you are doing over there? What are you going to become over there?" Listen my friend, if you have been faithful in the little things, if you have comforted yourself in the presence of God when no one else cared, I'm telling you: God is moving you from the rear to the forefront right now.

The Church needs to understand something about God. God doesn't throw anything away! God knows how to use the "fragments and scraps" of the human family. Since I raise dogs, every time my girls start to throw food away, I say, "Save the scraps!" They don't see any need for the food they don't want. It makes sense to them to discard what they don't need or want, but I know what my girls consider "scraps" is a vital source of food and life to my dogs. We are too quick to "scrap" and throw away the people who don't fit our needs or likes in life. God is saying to His Church family, "Save the scraps. I am going to make something out of the scraps!"

My masonry crews had just built up a wall to match the height of the other walls of a house when a rainstorm came. I thought the driving rain had ruined the wall with its fresh mortar and newly laid brick. I quietly said to the Lord, "Oh God, this entire wall is going to fall down." I sent the bricklayers home because the rain made it impossible for them to work.

We tried to cover up the wall and shield it from the rain, but the storm had already washed away mortar here and there. In my mind, it was almost a complete washout. I stayed around until the rain stopped and the wind calmed down, and my little nephew hung in there with me. Finally he looked at me and said, "Uncle Jeffrey, you want me to help you strike the wall?" He had learned some things about the construction trade, and particularly about masonry.

To a mason, the word "strike" refers to the work of removing excess mortar from the joints between bricks. In some cases, as with this wall that had been weakened by the rain, it also involves rechecking and strengthening all the joints, adding new mortar where necessary as well as removing excess mortar and reworking each joint to ensure strength and improve appearance.

I turned to him with a smile and said, "No sir. Any striking on this wall must be done by a professional. You see, you have to be very careful now because the wall is wet. It could easily collapse and cause serious injury." I appreciated my nephew's enthusiasm, but this job was even going to be a challenge for me, and I had done this kind of work for many years. Since the rain had passed and my crews had already been sent home, I began to strike the wall myself, not knowing how it would turn out. I carefully tooled it and swept the excess mortar off of the outer surfaces. It didn't look like much at this point, but it was still standing.

My young nephew had watched me strike the wall, and now I turned to him and said, "Well, tomorrow we will do something to this wall that we didn't do to any of the other walls. It is going to get some special attention." The next day, I put all my bricklayers on that wall.

After they washed and scrubbed it, that wall turned out to be the best wall on the job! Sometimes in life, you may begin "looking" just like everything or everyone else, but a storm of troubles or mistakes comes along to wash away or weaken everything that holds you together and makes you attractive to others.

After a storm of life messes you up, what happens next? The Bible describes what *should* happen: "Brothers, if someone is caught in a sin, you who are spiritual should restore him gently. But watch yourself, or you also may be tempted" (Gal. 6:1). I am glad the Lord has placed us in a family along with a multitude of brothers and sisters with a variety of gifts. Many times our faults or weaknesses can only be covered and restored by "a professional." There are situations in our lives where we don't need "amateurs" trying to "fix our wall."

Jesus Christ gave the Church special gifts in the form of apostles, prophets, evangelists, pastors, and teachers, who are specially equipped for special situations. I thank God for His specialists and seasoned professionals. God knew you were all messed up when He selected you. He knows what the storms have done in your life, so God won't just give you to "anybody" to fix you up. Don't be surprised when God puts you in the hands of a skilled servant of God to be restored.

He chose David also His servant, and took him from the sheepfolds: From following the ewes great with young He brought him to feed Jacob His people, and Israel His inheritance. So he fed them according to the

*integrity of his heart; and guided them by the skilful-
ness of his hands* (Psalm 78:70-72 KJV).

David restored the men at the cave of Adullam, and
led Israel and Judah "with the integrity of his heart,"
and he fed them with "the skillfulness of his hands."
Has God given you a leader with skilled hands and a
heart of integrity? You are no "throwaway" or "scrap"
in the eyes of God. You are His prize. He has selected
you to receive special attention, just like my bricklayers
gave some special attention to that storm-damaged
wall. Don't be surprised if you turn out to be one of the
strongest and most beautiful walls on the job—God has
selected you though others have rejected you.

God will sovereignly send you someone who is concerned about you because they can see that you are a
marred vessel in the Potter's hand. They will understand why you are unlovely today, and they will see with
God's eyes that you are destined to become beautiful
tomorrow in His hands. Though others may want to
discard you and hurry on to other prospects, God has
chosen to put you on His wheel. God will send you
someone who understands that you have been dropped
and kicked, overlooked, abused and misused. Put your
trust in God, and He will give you someone who is
equipped and anointed to give you some special attention because you are selected, not rejected.

I know you have been rejected by many, but God has
"contractors" in the Church who are trained and
equipped in the Spirit to restore the fallen, straighten

the bent, repair the damaged, and reclaim the discarded. When it is time to "put up extra wall ties," God's contractor doesn't go out and try to find somebody new to replace you. The God in him sees some value in you. He will take the time to pick you up and straighten you, saying, "What I have will do the job. I'm not going out to bring somebody else in."

God is raising up pastors and church leaders in this generation who will look over His flock and say, "What we have here will secure the wall. There are no scraps or throwaways in God's flock." The steps of your life are ordered by the God who carefully formed you in your mother's womb. It is no accident that you are reading these words because God ordained it! He knew this day would come, and He made it possible for you to hear about bent nails, chipped bricks, discarded cans, and an abandoned slave who helped David save his family. This isn't a statement about my value, it is a statement about *your value* and the *wisdom and purpose of God for your life*!

It is God who sent someone to pick you up where you had been abandoned in the field. God has sent someone to feed you when you were weak and ill. Your Creator has sent someone to your side with water because He knew you were thirsty. The Master Potter will provide a prophet with discernment who will know that you are on the wheel, and that you are only unlovely now because you are between what you were and what you shall be in Christ! God has taken you into His skillful hands to remake and remold you on His wheel into "another" to His liking.

I realize you may still feel "chipped" in your life, but the purposes of God can't be finished without you. Sure, you are still going through things in your life, but you need to take your place in the plan of God so it can move into its full glory. How is your sight? Have you clearly discerned that you are on the Potter's wheel, spinning between "it and another"?

Perhaps you don't understand why you are going through a trial. Just understand two things: You are in the Master's hand, and you are between your marred state and your restored state. God is making a new vessel out of you. He is recycling the valuable and the precious things He placed in you before your birth, and when His work is complete, you are going to be a column in His House!

God knows about the times you have been dropped. He knows you have been bent, but the most important news is that God is raising you up right now! You might as well get ready for things to change because you are between "it and another." You are still on the wheel, so expect your world to spin for awhile. Take courage and comfort in the one constant thing in your existence—the gentle, faithful, eternal touch of your Master's loving hands. You might be marred, but you're not in somebody's trash can or garbage heap—you're on the Master Potter's wheel.

You might be dysfunctional, but you're still on the wheel. You might be bent, but you have been selected by the Master Builder and He is straightening you out.

He refused to "replace" you because He made you one-of-a-kind, and only you will do. God is making you and fixing you because you can't do it yourself—you were never meant or equipped to do these things on your own. God is restoring and recycling you because He chose to, and He doesn't need anyone else's opinion on the matter!

God is giving you to people who know your potential by the Spirit of God. These people know your possibilities. They know you are going to be "another," a remade vessel fit for the Master's use. They understand the need to wait until you come off the Potter's spinning wheel because they have been on that wheel themselves!

God is fixing you right now—right in front of the devil. Of course the devil wants you to stop right now. He doesn't want you to reach your potential or make your possibilities realities. Who cares what he wants or thinks? You are in the Master's hands. Tell the devil, "I know where I am. You may say, 'Who are you? Why do you think you are anybody special? You are a failure!' But I say, 'So?! I'm going to become *another* after a while!' "

Remember that you are in good company. The moment God put you on His wheel, you joined a mighty family of great men and women who turned the world upside down *in spite of the fact* that they were despised, cast down, overlooked, abandoned, and ditched! Even though they didn't look like much, they did much! Tell your critics, cynics, and naysayers, "I may not look like much now, but 'So?!' Just wait until I come off the wheel!"

You may be saying, "I'm in battle with the enemy, and he doesn't want me to achieve the dream God gave me! He doesn't think I deserve to be in God's wall of life! He says there is no one who is crazy enough to give me special attention!" Just tell that old serpent, "So?! Didn't you forget something? I'm in the Potter's hands, and there is nothing you can do about it! He gave me my dreams. He put value and beauty in me. He thinks I deserve special attention. Who are you compared to the Giver of Life?"

God is sifting carefully through the sawdust and scrap piles of the house He is building. He is patiently gathering up all the nails together, whether they are straight or bent, new or used. He is even fixing the discarded pots no one else wants. God is gathering up all the discarded and so-called "empty" cans because He has a plan to recover the riches He invested in them! God is scrubbing the dirty discarded bricks that others have forgotten. He is sending out thousands of bricklayers and workers to gather up all the chipped bricks that have been discarded by society and people in the Church.

God is beating the trash man to the garbage dumpster because He knows there are riches and precious treasures hidden in the refuse piles of our generation. He is calling marred vessels to His wheel. He is assembling and laying all of the broken and dirty bricks because He wants to assemble a wall of "rejects-turned-selects" that will dazzle the world with its glory. He is assembling an army of dead men who will astound the world with His life in their new hearts.

Declare to yourself and those around you: "I'm going to be somebody. You might not know who I am, but I'm glad God knows who I am. I'm going through a recycling process. Yes, I'm in a restoration mode. You may not realize it, but I'm going to be *another* after a while! Just wait until I come off the Potter's wheel!"

You are reading this book because God is going to use you. He gives nothing to us simply for our use. Everything He gives us, He expects us to give away to others. If you are a bent nail, you can write this down and count on it: You will soon meet other bent nails who desperately need to hear about the miracle God worked in your life!

If God has sent you a man to pick you up from the wilderness where you were abandoned, then be prepared to be sent yourself. He has someone waiting in another deserted place who needs your helping hand and encouraging love to find life again. Once you are revived, you will be expected to lead others to victory and recovery in their lives!

Even God's Son experienced rejection and the difficulty of preparation. He submitted to a man and woman (his parents) for 30 years before He stepped into adult ministry. He submitted Himself to the timing of His Father. He submitted to the leading of the Spirit when He went to the wilderness, fasted for 40 days, and overcame the temptation of the devil. There were about five occasions in the Gospel of John leading up to the seventeenth chapter, when Jesus said, "My hour has not come yet." Yet "the time" came in the chapter 17 of John:

*Father, **the time has come**. Glorify Your Son, that Your Son may glorify You. ... And now, Father, glorify Me in Your presence with the glory I had with You before the world began* (John 17:1b,5).

Your "hour" was not here yesterday, but your hour has come now! God is ready to glorify you. The Greek word for "glorify" means "to put on display." Yes, you used to be bent, but God is straightening you out so He can put you on display where you will bring Him glory! You used to be a discarded slave going to waste in the fields of life. You were overlooked by anybody and everybody, but your hour has come now! God has an army in need of your help. He is ready to recover others, but He wants you to do your part. You are a key to the victory of others.

If this message strikes home and the Holy Spirit has spoken to your heart, then it is time to speak out and act on God's Word! Declare your desire and intentions. "I'm ready to be put on display! I was once a used and crumpled container that had been discarded after others thought all my usefulness had been drained and consumed. Now my value and worth have been recovered, and I am ready to be a column in the House of God! I used to be a bent nail buried under the refuse and trampled underfoot, but God has picked me up and I'm ready to be straightened out so I can be used in His House! I thought my remaining days would be spent in a forgotten ditch of life, but I'm ready to be picked up so I can dwell in the House of the Lord as a column of honor."

Now is the time. Your hour has come. There is nothing impossible for you because God says your hour has come! Pray, "Father, glorify me that I may glorify You!" Your Father was with you in your mother's womb, but after you were born and entered adulthood, you wandered far from His voice. Perhaps you went from barroom to barroom, or from woman to woman. Maybe you went from man to man or even church to church because you didn't know God's voice. Listen: Everything changed the day you heard your Savior's call. The hour has come for the humble to be elevated and exalted by God! It is your hour, the time has come to be promoted and to be placed on display by your proud and joyful Father.

When the ancient accuser of the brethren swaggers into your mind to point his finger and lay blame, declare the truth: "I'm in this wall now, and nobody can do anything about it! I'm chipped, but I'm still in God's hands. I'm marred, but I'm still in the Master Potter's hands! Yes, I make mistakes, but I'm still in His hands. Yes, I have faults, but I'm still in His hands! I know there are people who don't like me, but there were a lot of people who didn't like the Potter either—all I know is I am in His hands!"

This is your time, the hour God has ordained to place you on His wheel. You will soon be lifted from the wheel with a new look, a new feel, a fresh impression, and new shape carefully formed by His guiding hands. People will still try to declare that you will never succeed, but you are in His hands and far beyond the reach of mortal man or condemned devil. Yes, people will talk about you, but you are in His hands, and the words of man have no power over you. Jesus Himself spoke the only words you need to hear:

> *My sheep hear My voice, and I know them, and they follow Me: and I give unto them eternal life; and they shall never perish, neither shall any man pluck them out of My hand. My Father, which gave them Me, is greater than all; and no man is able to pluck them out of My Father's hand* (John 10:27-29 KJV).

You are in the hands of the Father and no man can pluck you out! No matter what man or devil may say, you are on your way to becoming *somebody* in God's Kingdom. Never forget to recognize the human vessels God will use to raise you back up on your feet! You couldn't do it without the men and women of God who dared to trust His voice and reach out to you. Thank God for the faithful people who believed in you in spite of your appearance or condition. These people are not only "Davids" sent to train you and transport you out of the caves of life and into the palace of your God-given potentials, but they are also "Josephs" who were sent ahead of you to preserve a posterity in the earth!

There is one final thing to remember if God sends along a Noah to build an ark to save you, or a Jacob who wrestles through the night on your behalf to change your name, though it dooms him to walk with a limp: Your destiny is written in their lives. *Another* has emerged from the struggle and the fight. A new redeemer and rescuer has just stepped off the Master Potter's wheel into the light—you were picked up, straightened, cleansed, and placed in the wall for such a time as this! Now go help others who are in the same plight. What was once the tail is now become the head. What was once last is now first. God helped you in your valley, now descend from the mountain to help others who have been discarded and left alone in the valley!